Dr. Angie Ward has written an incredibly [thoughtful and practical] book to help women understand the significance of calling. If the words *leader* and *calling* both exhilarate and paralyze you, Angie's words, stories, and insights will give you the peace and confidence to embrace your calling and step into the leader you are.

JENNI CATRON, author, speaker, and founder of The 4Sight Group

While reading *I Am a Leader*, I found myself wishing over and again that it had been written forty years ago, when I was starting my ministry journey. Angie addresses very practical, heartfelt issues of women in leadership. It is honest, balanced, and comprehensive in subject and will be a tremendous resource to any woman sensing God's call to lead.

REV. TAMMY DUNAHOO, VP of US Operations and general supervisor at The Foursquare Church

A smart and well-written master class in understanding and discovering your God-given calling. Filled with biblical insight, real-life examples, and articulate explanations of the often-confusing tensions of calling, Angie Ward's *I Am a Leader* is a must-read for every female leader longing to be all God is calling her to be!

KADI COLE, leadership consultant and author of *Developing Female Leaders*

This book is just what every woman in ministry struggling with calling and leadership needs. It is both biblical and balanced, powerful and practical, autobiographical and authentic, incisive and insightful, clear and creative, and humorous and helpful. Come to think of it, it's just what every Christian man needs, as well, both for himself and for more insight into the women around him. Thanks, Angie, for this special gift to all of us.

CRAIG L. BLOMBERG, PH.D., distinguished professor of New Testament, Denver Seminary

It shouldn't be so, but it often is. Christian women struggle to figure out their calling to lead because of implicit and explicit biases to the contrary. Ward's book is inspirational and practical, helping women understand the double meanings often layered on words like *ministry, calling,* and *leadership.* Using biblical examples, lots of women's voices, conversational questions, and great content, Ward guides the reader through the discernment process for women helping women be the gifted leaders God has freed them to be.

MARYKATE MORSE, woman leader, church planter, professor, and writer

I am thankful for leaders like Angie Ward who demonstrate and teach what it means to be a woman who leads within a biblical framework. Rather than getting bogged down in leadership limits, *I Am a Leader* helps women discover their unique calling and develop their God-given leadership gifts within that calling.

GEOFF SURRATT, cofounder of MinistryTogether and coauthor of *Together*

Angie Ward deftly navigates the minefield that women in leadership can sometimes face—touching on topics that most men never even have to consider. She answers questions such as, *Is it even okay for me to be a leader? How do I know what my calling is, and can I even use that term? How does my calling impact my children and my marriage? And what about various seasons of life?* For any woman who feels called to be a leader—in any sense of the term—Angie Ward invites you to walk into your God-given influence with dignity, authority, and grace for yourself and for every woman who will come after you.

AUBREY SAMPSON, author of *The Louder Song*, church planter, preacher, and part of Lausanne's Think Tank for Women in Leadership

Women often feel both a strong call from God and a strong hesitation. *I Am a Leader* is a practical resource that helps them name and navigate the concerns and step forward with confidence into the call. It provides stories and quotes throughout from a diverse collection of women, providing friends for the journey.

MANDY SMITH, pastor of University Christian Church; author of *The Vulnerable Pastor*

How qualified am I to speak about the calling of women into ministry? Well, technically, not very. But as a man who likes to think he's been a very small voice in the cheering section for women in leadership roles, I am so grateful for this book! Angie encourages her readers to step into the mysterious, beautiful, and not-always-easy life of following God's voice. But she never leaves you on the path alone and wondering. Like the greatest of coaches, Angie speaks with just the right mix of encouragement and nudging to keep things moving forward. Thoroughly biblical and utterly readable, this is a book I'll give to my daughters. And to more than a few men I know.

GREG HOLDER, lead pastor of The Crossing; author of *The Genius of One*

As a young woman exploring a career in ministry, this is a must-read. Angie's words remind me that my leadership gifts matter, while equipping me to negotiate the challenging aspects of exercising that calling at home and at work. Her holistic approach is full of grace and grit as she explores the *why* without ignoring the *how*. I know I will return to this book again and again. It is a blueprint for the balancing act of womanhood, work, and worship.

SAMANTHA BEACH KILEY, writer and performer

Read *I Am a Leader* and share in the stories of women finding their sense of God's call. Learn from the wisdom and depth of Angie Ward how to pray, discern, and see the signs of God moving in all seasons of your life. Turn these pages and experience "the nudge" of God's calling.

DAVID FITCH, B. R. Lindner chair of Evangelical Theology at Northern Seminary in Chicago; author of *Faithful Presence*

The whisper, the nudge, the prompting, that holy something . . . the calling. Angie has written a powerful, equipping resource to interpret that holy invitation in tangible ways. Read this book and step into the deep gladness of your calling.

TRICIA LOTT WILLIFORD, author of *You Can Do This* and *Just. You. Wait.*

Angie Ward's book, *I Am a Leader,* is the last leadership book you need to buy—man or woman. Yes, this book is written specifically for women and is spot-on in addressing the critical issues women need to face when accepting and pursuing their call. But a lot of the principles and wisdom shared is valuable for men as well. The chapter on "Stages of a Woman's Life" is masterful and really resonated with me as a developmental psychologist who counsels both women and men through the transitions in their lives. Ward doesn't just show you the city on the hill as a woman leader—she gives directions. If you are a woman, this is a *must-read* for you to be unleashed as a leader. If you are a man, *this book is a must read* to clear away the obstacles and champion the leader in the women the Lord has placed around you.

> **RODNEY L. COOPER, PH.D,** Kenneth and Jean Hansen Professor of Discipleship and Leadership Development at Gordon–Conwell Theological Seminary—Charlotte

For men, Angie's book should remind us that calling is not as simple as it should be for women. Yet it is simple. To use Angie's words, "You are unique;—and yet—You are not alone." My prayer is that Angie's stories and truth-telling will give a voice and a direction for women who know deep down that they are called, yet whose calling has not been welcomed. I join Angie in her prayer that women will take courage and be encouraged by her book.

> **TREY FINLEY, M.DIV.,** executive director of eleven:28 Ministries

Ward's writing is insightful, practical, and honest in ways that are not just enjoyable to read but also transformative. For all of us who desire that women would discover and live into their calling, this is simply one of the best resources around.

> **JR ROZKO,** national director of Missio Alliance

I AM A LEADER

WHEN WOMEN DISCOVER THE JOY OF THEIR CALLING

ANGIE WARD

A NavPress resource published in alliance
with Tyndale House Publishers

NavPress is the publishing ministry of The Navigators, an international Christian organization and leader in personal spiritual development. NavPress is committed to helping people grow spiritually and enjoy lives of meaning and hope through personal and group resources that are biblically rooted, culturally relevant, and highly practical.

For more information, visit www.NavPress.com.

CONTENTS

INTRODUCTION

It might feel like a nudge.

Or maybe it's a burden you can't shake.

A burning. A whisper. A leading. A feeling of discontent. A prompting. An invitation. Perhaps even a command.

It's hard to describe, but you're sure of it: You've experienced *something*.

This *something* has come from Someone outside of yourself, yet at the same time, it resonates deep within your spirit. And it is asking, perhaps urgently, for a response.

But . . . you have so many questions, all cluttering your head and heart, clamoring for attention.

Did I hear correctly? Can I really do this? How will I make this work? What will this mean for my family? What if I fail? What if I succeed?

You take a deep breath.

There it is, again.

Will you join me?

I know the feeling.

+ + +

I was twenty years old, at home in Wisconsin on Christmas break from my Christian college. An English/

Communications major with the goal of a journalism career, I was fortunate to work as a freelancer for my hometown newspaper. On this particular night, I was working my usual four-o'clock-to-midnight shift at the sports desk, fielding calls from high-school basketball coaches who were reporting that day's scores and stats. It was routine work, and I was hunched over my computer terminal when a voice interrupted my random thoughts.

"I want you to work *with* people instead of writing *about* them," the voice said.

And that voice was not coming from any other human in the newsroom.

I sat up straight. While I loved journalism, part of me was also interested in some type of Christian ministry. In fact, I had already declared a minor in Youth Ministry at college. As a teenager, I had been deeply impacted by my church's youth ministry and by my youth pastor and his wife, and I was interested in making a similar difference for teens. Still, my plan was to work as a reporter, eventually working my way up to a big-city newspaper or bureau, while maybe volunteering in youth ministry at a local church.

But by that Christmas break of my junior year, I had become jaded and cynical. Part of this was the result of getting up close to a lot of ugliness in the world as a journalist, but my cynicism was no doubt also fed by a growing anger toward what I saw as rampant hypocrisy among the Christians I knew. My "Christian" parents had just finalized an acrimonious divorce; my "Christian" church had split, resulting in the loss of four pastors in six months (including my youth pastor); and I saw all sorts of decidedly un-Christian activities among students and the administration at my "Christian" college.

I was seriously contemplating walking away from my faith—and then I heard that voice at the sports desk.

Mind you, I know that it is possible to work with people *and* write about them. But at that time in my life, I was using professional distance to protect myself from personal hurt. I thought that if I could keep a hard outer crust, I could avoid the potential pain of getting close to people. But when the voice spoke, I knew immediately what it meant for me.

I also knew immediately *who*—or rather, *Who*—was speaking. It was not the first time I had heard this voice. At the time, I was angry with God and hadn't been talking to him much, but I still knew when he was speaking to me— and this was one of those times. This invitation was not my first, although it was the first time I experienced clear direction from him about my vocation.

I didn't respond immediately to this voice, this *call*. First, I had to decide whether I was going to stick with the whole Christian thing in the first place. But over the course of the following year, this call to ministry became clear through a number of avenues of confirmation. My (eventual) response of humbled obedience began a nearly thirty-year ministry leadership journey that continues today.

THIS BOOK IS FOR YOU

If you are reading this book, you are part of a unique, more specific group of Christian women. You identify (or have been identified) as a *leader*, whether or not you currently serve in a formal leadership position within an organization. You are also involved in *ministry*: some type of specific Christian service, whether within a local church, a Christian ministry, your home, or your community—or even as a leader who is a Christian in an organization or context that is not explicitly Christian.

And at some point in your life, you have experienced a *call*: that nudge/burden/burning *something* that asks, *Will you join me?* And right now, you're wrestling with that invitation, that *calling*—what it is, and how it plays out for you.

Of course, these are a lot of loaded terms—words that can have varied meanings and powerful emotional connotations depending on your frame of reference. *Calling* is a loaded term. So is *ministry*. And, particularly for Christian women, so is *leader*.

So, what *is* calling, and how does a woman leader live it out? We'll get to that in-depth in the rest of this book. In addition to figuring out what calling *is*, we need to understand how to discern calling. Are there different types of calling? How do you know you're hearing an invitation from God and not just the rumblings of last night's pizza? And what does calling look like as it is lived out in real life and leadership—a woman's everyday responsibilities, issues of power and authority, family relationships? What about in various seasons of a woman's life, from young adulthood to empty nest? What role does money play in following a call? Where is the line between stepping out in faith or foolishness?

And then, of course, we must consider the challenges and curveballs women experience in pursuing their call. There are moments, months, or more when following a perceived calling involves great difficulty, disappointment, and pain. What do we do with doubt, discouragement, and dry seasons?

We'll get to all of that, I promise. But here at the beginning, it's helpful for us to first understand those other two loaded terms. What do we mean by *ministry*? And who qualifies as a *leader*?

What Counts as Ministry?

For many people, "the ministry" denotes full-time Christian service as either a pastor or a missionary. This understanding originated in medieval times, when a priest (the "sacred") was set apart to represent a congregation (the "secular") in prayers to God, preaching, and administering the sacraments.

The Reformation brought an emphasis on the priesthood of all believers—the idea that all Christians are equal in terms of access to God and ability to serve in his Kingdom mission.[1]

In other words, "There are no such things as spiritual and secular jobs—we just made that up," writes author and Bible teacher Jennie Allen. "God calls people to himself, and then to display him in every way, wherever we are. So are you called to teach or write or mother or build homes or fly planes? Beautiful. Do it as unto the Lord."[2] Christians are to be the hands and feet of Christ, ministering the gospel wherever God has placed them. Therefore, we should *all* be "in ministry."

Even if we do not subscribe to the sacred-secular divide, it is easy to rank certain types of Kingdom work as more important or spiritual. For example, we tend to rank full-time jobs over part-time jobs, paid positions over volunteer roles, overseas work over opportunities in our own town, and managers over worker bees. But as ministry leader and author Tish Warren Harrison rightly points out, "There is no task too small or too routine to reflect God's glory and worth."[3]

Serving as a missionary in Africa is ministry. So is pastoring a church. But when done for Christ, ministry is also washing dishes, foster parenting, teaching middle school, working a factory assembly line, folding laundry, performing surgery, waiting tables, balancing corporate ledgers, and bringing orange slices to Little League. As the apostle Paul wrote to the Colossians, "Whatever you do, work at it with all your heart, as working for the Lord, not for human masters" (Colossians 3:23).

Who Is a Leader?

We tend to think of leaders as those with a specific position or title within a formal organization. But the essence of leadership is *influence in relationship,* regardless of a particular title or role in a particular context.

In my seminary classes, I define leadership as "influence on people to movement toward a vision." By that definition, if you have any type of influence in any kind of relationship, you are a leader.

Let that sink in for a moment. *If you have influence, you are a leader.*

Again, we often think of influence in terms of someone "higher up" or "more important." But your influence can be gained or given from a number of sources: positional authority or title; financial, emotional, physical, or spiritual power;

or personal relationship and trust based on your example and integrity.

Influence is not restricted to a certain age, appearance, ability, ethnicity, socioeconomic status, or personality type. It can be exercised up, down, and all around wherever God has placed you.

So, yes, you are a leader if you are a CEO, a pastor, a director, a manager. But you are also a leader if you are an employee, a volunteer, a mentor, a discipler, a teacher, a writer, a friend, a neighbor, a wife, a mother, a daughter. The question is not *whether* you have influence; the questions are: *Where* do you have influence, and *how* are you using that influence to bring honor and glory to God?

HOW WE'RE GOING TO GET THERE

As I write this, I can see my fiftieth birthday a few swipes ahead on my calendar. Of that almost half a century, I have been a follower of Christ for nearly forty years and in some type of Christian ministry for almost thirty. I've served in volunteer and paid positions in churches, camps, campus ministries, and Christian colleges and seminaries. In those roles and now as a writer, teacher, and consultant, I've worked with hundreds of ministry leaders. I'm even married to a pastor, for Pete's sake.

In other words, the majority of my adult life has been spent in the realm of Christian ministry, listening for and responding to God's call. I, too, have wrestled—repeatedly—with issues regarding calling in general and my calling in particular: as a woman, a leader, a wife, a mom, and a follower of Christ. I have experienced confidence, clarity, confusion, discouragement, dry seasons, frustration, and fruitfulness. I'm certainly no expert; I'm just experienced to some degree, and I look forward to sharing more of my story as we walk together through the pages ahead.

You'll also find in this book the real-life experiences of women just like you and me. If I have any wisdom, it lies in the realization that there are many who are far wiser. In the following pages, you will meet dozens of amazing women of all ages, life stages, ethnicities, and geographic locations. I have been honored to hear and to hold their stories during the course of this project, and I am excited to introduce them to you in this book. Most of my conversations took place via video chat, with a few in-person meetings as geography allowed. In some of these stories, names have been changed to protect the privacy of individuals and organizations involved—but the stories and experiences are 100 percent true.

Friends, we're in this together. *We need each other.* This path of pursuing our calling is challenging enough without wondering and worrying whether our travel companions can be trusted. I want to make sure we're starting from the same place so that we know we can trust each other along the way. So, before we move forward, I'd like to lay out some assumptions and agreements.

First, the Bible is authoritative on all issues to which it speaks. It can be trusted because it is God's Word, and God is perfect and perfectly trustworthy. Not only does Scripture bear witness to itself and to the Messiah but there are plenty of other writings that establish the historicity of Jesus and the reliability of Scripture.

Second, we as humans are not perfect, nor are we perfectly trustworthy. Therefore, we can agree to disagree. The lenses with which we view the various issues related to a woman's calling are colored by our personal experiences, by our theological traditions, and by our cultural contexts. Yet we all tend to think our perspectives are the normal, "right" ones.

You might not agree with everything in this book. Even the women I interviewed would not always agree with each other if they met in person. But please know that every woman in these pages (including me) is a godly sister in Jesus Christ who seeks to follow him with her whole heart, soul, mind, and strength. Let's be open to what God might want to teach us through different perspectives.

Third, this book may make you uncomfortable. In fact, I hope it does. As a teacher, my goal is to create an environment that is safe, yet one that fosters *disequilibrium*: the uncomfortable feeling of instability or imbalance that is necessary for growth. Not only will you read stories that may not square with your own experiences or assumptions but you may feel God rocking your boat, moving you toward some type of change in attitude, belief, or action. I encourage you to pay attention, even to lean in to any discomfort you may feel. You may finish this book with more questions than answers, and that's okay. My desire is to help *you* wrestle with God's direction in your life, not to tell you what to do.

DEEP GLADNESS

The esteemed writer and theologian Frederick Buechner famously said that calling is "the place where your deep gladness and the world's deep hunger meet."[4] Pursuing your calling can often be very challenging. But there is unshakeable joy—deep gladness—to be found in the knowledge that you were made with a purpose and in the process of walking intimately with God to discover and live out that purpose as a woman leader.

My hope and prayer is that as you read this book, you will experience the power and deep gladness of these two truths:

1. You are unique;

—and yet—

2. You are not alone.

You are unique. There is no one else exactly like you. You have been "fearfully and wonderfully made" (Psalm 139:14) as "God's handiwork, created in Christ Jesus to do good works, which God prepared in advance for [you] to do" (Ephesians 2:10). As a leader, you are an even rarer breed of Christian woman. I hope this book helps you discover, clarify, and rejoice in your unique story, gifts, and calling.

At the same time, you are not alone. There are women who have walked the same path before you, and there are women around the world who walk beside you. I hope this book deepens your sense of the powerful, beautiful sisterhood we all share as Christ-following, female ministry leaders.

Let's step into this together, shall we?

CONTINUE THE CONVERSATION

» Why did you decide to read (or at least start!) this book?

» What are you hoping to learn from this book?

» Ask the Lord to open your mind and heart to what he might want to teach you as you progress through these pages.

» Would you describe your journey of calling as one of "deep gladness"? If not, how would you describe it?

Chapter 1

WHAT IS CALLING?

I can't remember when I first heard the term *calling*. I just know that by the time I got to seminary at age twenty-four, I was using the word to describe why I was there and why I picked the particular seminary I attended.

Why did I come to this seminary? Simple. "God called me here," I replied, to knowing nods and murmurs.

By then, I had marinated in Christian subculture for long enough that I think the word had just seeped into my vocabulary. Growing up in church, I heard missionaries talk about how they were called to specific countries and people groups. I heard my pastors talk about how they had been called to (or away from) our church. In college, I probably heard chapel speakers talk about the importance of following God's call. I also talked with friends who had been dumped by a boyfriend or girlfriend who felt God "telling" them to do it. (Of the validity of that last "calling," I was often skeptical.)

As a Christian, *calling* definitely seemed like a super-spiritual word. A "call" from God implied a close relationship with him. Who wouldn't want to hear from God directly? Plus, using the word *calling* raised the speaker and his or her behavior above dispute. How do you argue with someone who claims to act on the voice of the Lord?

As I continued through seminary and then into vocational ministry, I heard and used *calling* frequently. I heard it used in so many ways, however, that I wasn't actually sure what it meant. And as I progressed through different stages of my own life, I continued to wrestle with calling: both what it was in general and what *mine* was.

So, what *is* calling, really? Can it be defined? Are there different types of calling? And how is God's "calling" (whatever that is) related to his commands, our "purpose" or "vocation," our passions and dreams, and our everyday responsibilities?

WHEN GOD CALLS

The theme of calling is woven throughout God's Word, although it sometimes looks a bit different than we'd expect. The Hebrew word commonly translated *called* in English had two primary meanings: either to catch someone's attention or to name a person or place.[1] For example, an aging Isaac *called* for his son Jacob to come receive his blessing (Genesis 28:1), while a few verses later, Jacob renamed the city of Luz, *calling* it Bethel ("house of God") after seeing God in a dream near that city (Genesis 28:19).

WOMEN SPEAK: BIBLICAL CHARACTERS

Which biblical character and his or her calling has inspired you?

- "Priscilla, because her calling and function in the church are easy for me to identify with. She's a married, working woman whose calling and function in the church were influential and necessary for its health." —*Amanda*

- "Jonah, because my first instinct is to sometimes run the other direction when God calls me to something challenging. How many days have I been in the belly of a whale, avoiding my own Nineveh?" —*Allison*

- "Peter. He was such a mess-up, and I can so relate. I love that Jesus' call on Peter's life didn't change after he fell and failed."—*Nicole*

- "Job. I love how God let him ask hard questions."—*Tricia*

- "Esther. I hate confrontation, but God repeatedly puts me in positions of power or leadership to be a mouthpiece for change."—*Kelly*

- "Priscilla. I love that she was bold, intelligent, and strategic and that she operated as part of a team." —*Jana*

- "Deborah, because she made herself available to be used by God, and he did just that."—*Jennifer*

Of course, these types of calling in Scripture were not limited to human-to-human interaction. Many times in the Old Testament, we see God communicating directly with human beings. In the book of 1 Samuel, God spoke to Samuel, a young minister-in-training under Eli the priest. One evening, Samuel seemed to hear an audible voice calling his name, so he ran to Eli's side, assuming the priest had summoned him. But Eli said no, he had not called for the boy, and Samuel should go back to bed.

After this happened three times, the wise old priest realized that Samuel was hearing the voice of the Lord. He instructed the boy, "Go and lie down, and if he calls you, say, 'Speak, LORD, for your servant is listening'" (1 Samuel 3:9). Samuel did as he was told, and thus began his lifetime of listening to the Lord as a prophet to the kingdom of Israel.

The Bible also shows us numerous examples of groups and individuals who were chosen by God—"called out," as it were—for a specific role or task. In the Old Testament, one way God commonly did this was by command. For example, to Abram (later Abraham), God's direction was firm and clear: "Go from your country, your people and your father's household to the land I will show you" (Genesis 12:1).

Although the biblical description of this interaction does not use the word *called*, both the Lord and the Jewish people later referred to it as an example of calling. Centuries later, God told the Israelites through Isaiah, "Look to Abraham, your father. . . . When I called him he was only one man, and I blessed him and made him many" (Isaiah 51:2). And the writer of the New Testament letter to the Hebrews also noted Abraham's calling as part of the "Faith Hall of Fame":

By faith Abraham, when called to go to a place he would later receive as his inheritance, obeyed and went, even though he did not know where he was going.

HEBREWS 11:8

Other well-known Old Testament examples of God calling an individual via command include Noah, Moses, Joshua, Gideon, Isaiah, Jeremiah, and Jonah.

In the Old Testament, God established a covenant relationship with the chosen nation of Israel and called individuals out of that nation for specific work. Jesus demonstrated a very different approach in the New Testament. A call from Jesus began not with a command for a task but with a simple invitation: "Follow me." As the Son of God, Jesus sought first to draw people to the Father through himself. This invitation was open to all individuals, regardless of nationality.

An invitation to give up everything to follow Jesus was also an invitation to join him in the work of the Kingdom. "Follow Me, and I will make you fishers of men," Jesus said to Peter and Andrew (Matthew 4:19, NASB). As his followers continued to grow in knowledge and faith, Jesus sent them on his behalf to heal the sick, drive out demons, and proclaim the Kingdom of God (Luke 9:1-6; 10:1-17).

After Jesus' ascension to heaven, his followers continued to preach and practice this understanding of calling, first as an invitation to follow Jesus ("come") and then as an imperative to serve him ("go"). The early church also recognized that each person was given specific abilities, resources, and opportunities to be used in service to God. We see an example of this in

Acts 6, when the believers chose seven men to care for widows so that the apostles could focus on teaching the Word of God.

It makes sense that calling would be a recurring theme in the writings of Paul, as his story is perhaps the most famous New Testament example of calling. After a dramatic encounter with God, this man known as Saul, a notorious persecutor of Christians, became Paul, follower of Christ. In Acts 13, the Lord—through the Holy Spirit—instructed leaders at the church in Antioch to "set apart for me Barnabas and Saul [as he was still known] for the work to which I have called them" (verse 2). Paul ended up becoming the greatest missionary of the first century, spreading the gospel and starting over a dozen churches throughout the Roman empire. In his letters and his preaching, Paul repeatedly referenced his calling as an apostle and evangelist to the Gentiles (Romans 1:1; 1 Corinthians 1:1), noting that he was "sent not from men nor by a man, but by Jesus Christ and God the Father" (Galatians 1:1).

In the lives of a host of men and women—Job, Joseph, Esther, the prophets, John the Baptist, Mary, Peter, Philip, Priscilla, Lydia, Timothy, to name only a few—the Lord chose, invited, or directed people for a specific purpose. Even when the word itself is not used or God does not speak directly, the *concept* of calling clearly permeates Scripture.

DEFINING CALLING

In Scripture, *calling* is a broad and encompassing concept, but in the centuries following the early church, the term began to take on a narrower meaning: that of ordained service specifically to the church. One contemporary ramification of this historical shift is that the term *call* now has a specific definition and use in some church denominations. In these circles, a call is generally understood as an invitation to pastor a church. A "called position" requires a personal sense of "call" by the minister, a confirmation of that individual's call by the denominational governing body, and an actual "call" (or invitation) by the congregation to a specific position within that church. As you can imagine, the variety of uses of the concept and term *calling* between various denominational and theological understandings makes for confusing conversations!

So, how can we define calling for the purposes of this book? One of my doctoral professors once said, "The person who controls the definition controls the discussion." Since we're going to spend the rest of this book discussing what calling looks like in real life, we should try to find a simple yet clear definition to make sure we're starting from the same place. But calling is something known as a *construct*—an intangible, often hypothetical concept, like human intelligence, happiness, or initiative—that is difficult to define or quantify. Here are how some others have tried to capture calling:

> The truth that God calls us to himself so decisively
> that everything we are, everything we do, and
> everything we have is invested with a special
> devotion and dynamism lived out as a response
> to his summons and service.—Os Guinness[2]

> Individuals' calling to partnership with God in
> which particular gifts are evoked and developed in

concert with their discernment of the particular role
God has given them to play during a certain period
of their lives.—Richard Robert Osmer[3]

A conviction [that] steadily deepens.—L.T. Lyall[4]

A strong urge towards a particular way of life or
career.—*Oxford Living Dictionaries*[5]

[Calling] at its deepest level is, "This is something
I can't not do."—Parker J. Palmer[6]

Looking at the definitions above, we can't miss the consistent theme of *conviction*—an inner persuasion, in this case
toward a particular life direction, that cannot be ignored. If
we follow Christ, both the conviction and the direction are
given by God.

But conviction isn't the whole sum of calling. I think that
good ol' Webster's dictionary actually defines it best:

calling (*n.*): a strong inner impulse toward a particular
course of action especially when accompanied by
conviction of divine influence.[7]

So let's apply some algebraic simplification principles and
move terms around to put all of these things together:

*Calling is a God-given conviction about your life's
direction.*

WOMEN SPEAK: DEFINING CALLING

How would you define calling?

- "I have always thought of calling as a sense of 'I can do no other.'"—*Fran*

- "I would define *calling* as my specific assignment, my place to be in the body."—*Chara*

- "Calling is the way God has asked each person to live out their faith in ways consistent with their giftings and place in life."—*Tammi*

- "For me, calling is that deep-down voice of God that says, 'This is what you were made for.'"—*Cherie*

- "Calling is when you realize God's plan for your life. That's when you can see how you've been groomed and gifted for following it."—*Allison*

- "I would define *calling* as a drawing to a personal vision or a certain job, purpose, or mission."—*Joyce*

- "Calling is the Holy Spirit's interference with one's regular way of life, followed by an invitation to do something different."—*Denise*

As we will see throughout this book, a person's calling can take many forms. But at its core, calling comes from God, it involves a deep inner assurance, and it has the potential to change the course of a person's life. Calling is powerful stuff.

No wonder so many people spend so much time and energy trying to discern theirs.

THE NATURE OF CALLING

Calling is powerful. It is also complex, which is why it can be so hard to understand and discern. In my attempts to understand (and explain) calling, I have discovered that calling has a both/and characteristic as well as several either/or possibilities.

Both/And

As we have seen, the New Testament speaks of a dual sense of calling: first of a call to follow Christ, and then of a call to personally join his work in the world. Writers and theologians use various terms for this dual sense of calling, including "general and specific," "primary and secondary," "ordinary and special," or "vertical and horizontal." Writer Halee Gray Scott explains the distinction in this way: "We are first called into the family of God; then we are called out into the world to bring others into a relationship with God."[8]

In this sense, as author and social critic Os Guinness points out, "No follower of Christ is without a calling."[9] *However, it is important to keep these callings in the correct order.* "The calling to follow Christ lies at the root of every other calling," explains the Theology of Work Project.[10] "Secondary callings matter, but only because the primary calling matters most."[11] Guinness's point cannot be overstated: *The most important calling is Jesus' invitation to follow him.* If you have not accepted this invitation, no other calling matters.

This primary call to follow Christ also involves a fundamental shift in identity. By answering this call, we become legally adopted, fully vested sons and daughters of God (see Romans 8:14-17). The follower of Jesus is therefore "called" in two ways: first, by being invited to follow; and second, by receiving a new name and identity in Christ—which takes us back to the basic meaning of the biblical word for calling.

Thirteen years before I heard my secondary call at the sports desk in the newsroom, I heard God's primary call on a Sunday morning at church. It was Palm Sunday 1979, just before my ninth birthday. I don't remember many details of the sermon by our senior pastor, but I do know that something stirred deep in my young heart when he talked about going to heaven and living with Jesus forever. As was a regular practice at that church, at the end of his sermon, the pastor gave an "altar call," an invitation to come to the front of the sanctuary to pray to trust Christ for salvation.

Although I was painfully shy as a child and the thought of going forward in church terrified me, I nevertheless felt like this was something I wanted—no, *needed*—to do. I nudged my mom and asked if she would go with me. She agreed, and I self-consciously slipped from the pew and into the aisle. A deacon met us at the railing bordering the steps at the front of the sanctuary, knelt with us, and asked if I knew what I was doing and its significance. I nodded, my stomach churning with nerves. He kindly offered to pray first, and I could repeat what he said. I don't remember any of the words we prayed; my stomach continued revving, faster and faster, until the deacon and I said, "Amen."

And then I threw up, right there on the altar at the front of the church.

It's true: Jesus cleansed me from the inside out.

In that very public, projectile moment at the front of our church, I not only professed belief, I *became* a new person, one now identified by my relationship to Christ.

Each of us who follows Jesus has received a primary calling to a new identity, but this calling is not just individual. I believe Guinness correctly expands the notion of general calling to include what he labels a "corporate" calling: "The corporate calling . . . is that part of our life-response to God that we undertake in common with all other followers of Christ," he writes.[12]

In other words, there is a thick, oft-neglected middle layer of obedience between general and specific callings. In our Western individualism, we can easily jump from responding to Christ's initial invitation to trying to figure out our personal purpose. We worry about finding our specific call while ignoring so many general things God *has* already called us toward.[13] As members of the church (the universal body of Christ), all Christians are called—actually, commanded—to Christlikeness in a variety of everyday actions and attitudes: caring for the poor, widows, and orphans; demonstrating the fruit of the Spirit; living in right relationships; and showing faithfulness in the myriad of "little things" that have been entrusted to our stewardship.

Julie, a recent seminary graduate at age forty-four, found it helpful to focus on her corporate calling and on *being* while she waited on direction for *doing*. "A few months ago, I had a conversation with the professor who has mentored me," she shared. "As I was struggling with where to go from here, he encouraged me by saying he was not convinced that it was so much 'what I was going to do' as 'who I am everywhere I go' that God was going to use. That's not to say I won't 'do' something but that I shouldn't get fixated on it."

As Guinness declares, "Anyone citing his or her individual calling as grounds for rejecting the church's corporate calling is self-deluded."[14] We are wrong to expect God to reveal our specific calling if we do not first seek to obey this corporate calling.

It is crucial for us to understand our primary calling, both corporate and individual, before we can truly live into our secondary calling. But where the primary calling is clear and defined, the secondary calling can feel more elusive. Because of that, for the remainder of this book, when I talk about *calling* and the process of discovering and living out your calling, I will be talking about the specific or secondary calling to join God's redemptive work in the world, not the primary or general calling to follow Christ.

Either/Or

As we respond to God's primary calling, we should remain attentive and open to how God may choose to reveal our secondary calling. We may find that our calling emerges in ways that are different from what we expect or from how it has emerged for others. There are several either/or methods by which God might reveal a secondary calling: broad or detailed, patient or urgent, time-limited or long-term.

BROAD OR DETAILED

In the actual delivering of an individual call, God sometimes gives us details up front. Other times, the initial instruction is more general, and he gives us the details as we go. To Jonah,

God's initial direction was specific: Go to Nineveh (Jonah 1:2). For Abraham, it was more general: Leave your family and go to the land *I* will show you (Genesis 12:1). Paul's broader call was to proclaim the gospel as a missionary to the Gentiles (Acts 9:15; Romans 11:13), and as he followed that call, he received specific instructions regarding where to travel and how long to stay. We see examples of both broad and detailed callings in Scripture, so both are equally viable divine methods. God knows that sometimes we need the details and sometimes we need to learn trust while we wait for the details.

"At the moment, I think my calling is just to be at seminary," said Sharon, who is pursuing a master of divinity in Christian Formation. "I don't know exactly where it goes beyond that, and I think that's by God's design, because he knows I like to think I have control of my life. I think this is probably a period of obedience, just to follow step one and let steps two, three, and four kind of coalesce as they may."

Jes reported a similar experience. "Starting in the fall of 2016, I felt like God wanted me to quit my job," she said. "I thought, 'Well, I'll quit when I know what to do.' But God said, *No*. He called me to quit and just wait. The way he deals with me is to give me one tiny glimpse at a time."

This broad-or-detailed aspect of calling can also apply to roles and direction, not just to timetable. Some Christ followers are called to a specific country, people group, job, position, or organization; others are called to a general type of ministry, wherever or to whomever God leads.

During a focused period of discernment about twenty years ago, I sensed God clarifying that my broad calling was to "identify, develop, and encourage ministry leaders." God has led me to exercise that calling in a variety of contexts and roles at different times in my life. I've served as a volunteer and a paid staff member; in churches, Christian colleges and seminaries, nonprofit ministries, and my own home; with youth and adults, women and men; in the United States and abroad; and through writing, teaching, speaking, leading, coaching, and consulting. Sometimes I've had a formal role, and many other times, I have done these things without an official position or title.

If God doesn't give you the details, it does not mean that your calling is less legitimate—or less worthy of obedience. "When God tells you to follow Him, He is not obligated to reveal your destination immediately," writes pastor and author Henry Blackaby.[15] Our job is to follow what we *have* been given, not to worry about what we have not yet heard.

PATIENT OR URGENT

For some, God's calling begins as a gentle nudge or a distant vision. Other times, his calling interrupts life like a fire alarm, jolting you to attention and immediate action. Joseph, the son of Jacob, dreamed as a young boy that his brothers would bow down to him. He was subsequently sold into slavery and languished in prison for years while God orchestrated the location, timing, and connections that one day would turn Joseph into the second-most-powerful man in Egypt, ready to lead the country and its neighbors—including his groveling brothers—through a devastating famine (Genesis 37, 42–45). Joseph, the father of Jesus, on the other hand, received orders—also in a dream—to take Mary and young Jesus and leave Bethlehem immediately for Egypt in order to hide from King Herod, who was seeking to kill the boy (Matthew 2:13-15). Moses underwent a forty-year (!) season of preparation before encountering God in the burning bush (Exodus 7:7; Deuteronomy 34). Paul received a plea from a man of Macedonia via a vision and got ready to leave at once, believing it was the Lord's direction (Acts 16:9-10).

My friend LeeAnn was happily following what she felt was God's calling to serve and lead in a Bible study for medical wives in her city of Rochester, Minnesota, home of the world-famous Mayo Clinic. But there was another nudge that wouldn't go away—the nudge to adopt a child with special needs. "I always felt like, being in Rochester, we had this overwhelming sense of—not obligation, but like, here we are with great insurance, ten minutes from one of the major medical centers in the world," LeeAnn said. "The more I found out about the need for adopting, the more my reasons [for not adopting] were cheapened.

"It became something that was simmering for a while. I could put the lid on the pot to stop it, but then it boiled over. Everything I was studying and reading just became overwhelming," she continued. "I thought, *We have room in our house, and we have room in our hearts—how can we not?*" LeeAnn, her husband, Peter, and their two teenage daughters adopted a girl with spina bifida from China. A year later, they added a boy with similar medical issues.

"There was *huge* fear amid all the unknowns," LeeAnn admitted. "But being on the 'I can't do it' side is just as stressful as taking that step of faith when the Spirit is pushing."

The timetable God uses to reveal his calling should not affect our timetable—or our willingness—to obey that calling. The Bible tells us, "With the Lord a day is like a thousand years, and a thousand years are like a day" (2 Peter 3:8). We need to trust his timing and be ready to respond as soon as the calling becomes clear.

TIME-LIMITED OR LONG-TERM

God's calling can also vary in duration. Some may be called to a particular task for a very short time period, others to a lifetime assignment. Shortly after Saul's conversion on the road to Damascus, God gave a very specific calling to a disciple named Ananias: "Go to the house of Judas on Straight Street and ask for a man from Tarsus named Saul, for he is praying. In a vision he has seen a man named Ananias come and place his hands on him to restore his sight" (Acts 9:11-12). Ananias's obedience to this time-limited calling brought sight to Saul, who then took the gospel to the Gentiles.

The Old Testament prophets and the New Testament apostles usually received a long-term calling, with short-term assignments as part of that long-term call. The prophet Jeremiah received a word from the Lord that he had been set aside before birth as a prophet to the nations (Jeremiah 1:5). He then received dozens, perhaps hundreds, of short-term messages and instructions over the course of his prophetic life.

Sometimes a time-limited calling opens doors and desires for a longer-term opportunity or serves as preparation for the long-term calling, or vice versa. The Bible doesn't tell us a lot about Esther's everyday responsibilities as queen to King Xerxes, but we do know that she was in the right position at the right time when Haman developed a plot to kill her Jewish countrymen and women. Esther's marriage to the king (her long-term calling) allowed her to approach him in a time of crisis (a short-term calling) and ask him for an addendum to the murderous edict so that the Jews could defend themselves.

Of course, God can use these same type of "doorways" today. Andrea had grown up as a missionary kid, living in Ireland and the Philippines for seven years. Despite that (or perhaps because of it), she informed God, "I'll do short-term trips, but I won't do long-term trips." (You can see where this is going, can't you? Never say "never" to God . . .) A few years later, as a high-school junior, Andrea was back at her family's home church in the United States, singing and worshiping at a youth-ministry event, when God first planted the seeds for her calling.

"I remember praying, 'God, I want to follow your will for my life,'" she explained. "Then I felt God say, 'I want you to go into missions.' I freaked out. I was bawling. I was like, 'No, absolutely not.'" A year later, however, she went with her youth group on a short-term mission trip to Nicaragua. "That is when God started to break down those walls and show me that maybe life as a full-time missionary isn't the worst thing in the world, and how my passion for education, and math education specifically, could fit into ministry in Nicaragua," she said. Andrea ended up going to Nicaragua for nine more short-term trips before moving there as a full-time missionary, teaching math at a Christian school. "This is home now," she said.

An attorney in what she calls her "former life," Carolyn began working at her church ten-to-fifteen hours per week, developing the small-group ministry in order to help fix a problem she had experienced: trying to connect at a church of over three thousand attendees. "Fast-forward over time, and that little part-time gig turned out to be a calling and a career," she said. "Every year, I ask God, 'Really, we're doing this another year?'" Carolyn is now pastor of small groups and a core member of her church's pastoral team, which includes additional responsibilities and authority in the areas of hospital visitation, message planning, curriculum writing, and worship planning, among others.

"When I was in my twenties, I thought calling was this big 'aha,' like finding the person you marry or something," said Carolyn, now fifty. "Calling is really just following Jesus into whatever he is asking you to do in that season of life."

These stories show that God can call us in any way he wants, to anything he wants. He may call us to a purpose, a posture, a path, a group of people, or a specific position. Our responsibility is to develop listening ears and obedient hearts for whatever God wants to reveal, in whatever ways he chooses to reveal it.

SORTING THROUGH TERMS

As you read this, you may feel that *calling* sounds a lot like some other words and ideas you've heard related to your life direction, such as *purpose* or *responsibilities* or *passions*. How does *calling* connect to the other terms and concepts that are part of a Christian's life?

Purpose

In 2002, Pastor Rick Warren of Saddleback Church in Southern California launched a worldwide phenomenon with his bestselling book *The Purpose Driven Life*. "Even before the universe was created, God had you in mind, and he planned you for his purpose," Warren writes.[16] To date, *The Purpose Driven Life* has sold over thirty *million* copies, making it one of the top-ten bestselling Christian books of all time.[17] The whole idea of personal purpose clearly touched a nerve with Christians and non-Christians alike.

So, how does *purpose* relate to *calling*? I believe they are very similar; in fact, Os Guinness uses the terms interchangeably. When most people talk about purpose, however, they are usually referring to the idea of *personal* or *specific* calling, not the general calling to Christ or even the corporate calling toward Christlikeness. *Purpose* can be a great substitute word for the idea of a specific calling, and in many contexts, it may be a better word to start a conversation instead of the churchy-sounding word *calling*. (I doubt *The Calling Driven Life* would have been a bestseller.) Just be clear about how you are using *purpose* in light of the various meanings and layers of *calling* that we have explored, and don't ignore the spiritual importance of general and corporate callings over and above your personal calling.

Vocation

In contemporary conversation, the word *vocation* is often used synonymously with *occupation* or *career*. For example, the term *vocational ministry* usually refers to *occupational* ministry, such as a paid pastoral position in a church. *Vocation* is more correctly translated as "calling," however: the former comes from the Latin root for *voice*, while the latter comes from the Anglo-Saxon root for the same concept.[18] In his book *Let Your Life Speak: Listening for the Voice of Vocation*, Parker Palmer equates the two terms, noting that vocation is not a goal to be pursued, but a calling to hear[19] and "a gift to be received."[20]

Needs

A wise children's-ministry director at a former church once told me, "Not every need constitutes a call." She meant that just because the nursery needed more workers did not mean that it was my responsibility to fill that need. As followers of Christ and as leaders, however, we should always keep our eyes open to the obvious needs around us and for ways we might meet those needs. "There is a time and a place to search for our unique parts in God's story," writes Jennie Allen, "*but* . . . here is my admonition: Respond to the need you see. *Right now.*"[21]

Also, never, *ever* develop the attitude that a particular task or need is beneath you. As part of your corporate calling as a servant of Christ, be willing to do whatever needs to be done.

Responsibilities

Responsibilities require our *response*. Sometimes we choose our responsibilities, and sometimes they are put on us. Either way, our responsibilities must be our first priority—our first calling, as it were.

If you are married, if you have children, if you are caring for an aging parent, if you are employed, if you have made some other type of commitment—take care of your responsibilities, for in doing so, you are fulfilling your calling. "The genuine call of duty and the voice of God do not conflict," writes J. Oswald Sanders. "It is our duty to do our duty. That simple fact takes care of a large area of life for which no further guidance need be sought."[22]

The Bible is clear that we are to be faithful in the little things (Luke 16:10)—and our various responsibilities often require a lot of little things. But it is in these little things that our faith and our faithfulness are forged. "The crucible of our formation is in the monotony of our daily routines," Tish Harrison Warren wisely writes in her book, *Liturgy of the Ordinary*.[23] In other words, your responsibilities aren't in the way of your calling; they are a big part *of* your calling.

Dreams and Passions

We will look more at the roles of dreams and passions in the next chapter, but I'll admit that I get a bit nervous when I hear those words used in the context of calling. In our culture, we often hear how we should follow *our* dreams and passions. However, true calling is an invitation to respond *to God*. Dreams and passions are great—God can plant them in our minds and hearts as part of the calling process—but not all of our dreams or passions automatically equate to a God-given calling.

CALLING AND LEADERSHIP

What is the relationship between leadership and calling? While each of us has influence, not every woman is cognizant of or intentional about that influence. Among those who are, however, leadership is a critical part of their *identity*. They may also have a leadership role or title, but they view themselves as leaders regardless of any particular position or rank on an organizational chart. It's just who they *are* because of how they see the world and their place in it.

Leadership, then, can be a calling to a role, but it can also be a calling to responsibility as a person of some type of influence. I am a leader—I view myself as a person of potential influence, and others automatically view me that way as well—even in situations where I don't have a formal leadership role and no one knows anything about me. For me, and for many other women leaders, *women* is an adjective that colors and informs my identity as a leader. I'm not a woman who happens to have a leadership role; *I am a leader* who happens to be a woman.

This is a critical distinction, and it explains why many woman leaders (including myself) don't always feel they "fit" within women's traditional ministry roles or expectations. Given the unique challenges that women leaders face, they (we) may sometimes feel they are a leader "trapped" in a woman's body, struggling to figure out how to faithfully live out this part of their identity. It might be helpful for you to reflect on the nature of your own leadership calling. And as we continue our journey together through this book, keep in mind that this leadership identity provides an overlay to any other role to which God may call you.

WHAT NOW?

So what does all of this mean for you and me as women ministry leaders?

First, *you have been called.*

This calling begins with an invitation to follow Christ. It then extends to the corporate calling of Christlikeness, then to your personal responsibilities, and finally, to a more specific God-given conviction—a "special" or "secondary" calling—regarding your life's direction.

Take a few minutes to sit with this truth: *You have been called.*

The God of the universe speaks to us. He catches our attention. He asks us to follow him. He gives us a new identity. And to top it all off, he invites us to join his work in the world. That's a whole lot of love at work, right there.

If you gain nothing else from this book, I hope you at least take away a deeper sense of God's love for you. His calling is not about fear, force, or coercion; it's about his bottomless love.

Second, *there is no one-size-fits-all calling* when it comes to a person's "specific" call. God can call any person to any number of things, using any number of ways. Many of the women I talked to for this book prefaced their stories with, "For me . . ." to clarify that their experience was personal and not prescriptive.

Because each woman's calling is unique, we should never let ourselves fall into the trap of comparing callings. No calling from God is better, more important, or more spiritual than another. God has created each one of us for a special role. Instead of comparing, we should focus instead on clarifying—seeking God's direction about our own calling and helping other women discover theirs.

KINGDOM WOMEN ARE DIVERSE

We are kingdom women, and we are diverse. We have short hair and we have long hair; dirt is under our fingernails from toiling under the sun, and our fingernails are nicely manicured with pink nail polish; we stay at home with the children, care for our husbands, and support their careers, but we also choose to wear blue pantsuits and pastor churches. We wear yoga pants, leggings, mom jeans, cargo shorts, long skirts, and daisy dukes. . . .

We have gifts to teach, preach, prophesy, serve, lead, and build. We are church planters, we are kitchen ladies, we are number crunchers, we are directors, and we are worship leaders. We are nurturing, we are assertive, we are maternal, and we are fierce. . . . Many have tried to box us in or tell us who we *should be*, but when we look to Christ, we see cruciformity, love, grace, courage, and presence. Sure, try to box us in, but we are kingdom women, and we are diverse.[24]

Tara Beth Leach

CONTINUE THE CONVERSATION

» How has your denominational or theological background shaped your understanding of calling?

» How did you experience God's general (or primary) call to follow him?

» Are you obeying God in the "middle layer" between your general and your specific calls? In what areas do your attitudes and actions need to better reflect Christ?

» To whom are you most tempted to compare your calling? Why? Ask God to help you give up any internal need for comparison.

» Name some biblical characters who learned only the broad direction of their call at the beginning, and others who received more details up front.

» What are your current responsibilities? Are you tending to them faithfully?

Chapter 2

DISCERNING A CALL

"How did you end up doing what you do now?"

It's a question I hear frequently as I travel, teach, and speak to ministry leaders. Often, the real question behind that question is one about calling, and about the questioner's calling in particular. The question behind "How did you end up here?" is actually "How did you discover your calling?" And the question behind *that* is "How do *I* discover *my* calling?"

The answers—to all three questions—take a bit of time to explain and unpack. I will answer the first two questions throughout this book as I tell more of my story. This chapter focuses on the third question. How can you discern God's calling for *your* life? By what methods does God reveal a call? Is there anything you can do to help that process? And how do you know you are truly hearing God, not just the bad sushi you had for lunch?

According to a 2013 Barna survey, "only 40 percent of practicing Christians say they have a clear sense of God's calling on their lives."[1] If you are fortunate to be counted among them, I hope this chapter confirms the calling you have already experienced. And if you are among the other 60 percent, I hope this chapter helps bring you clarity about your own calling as we explore the process of discernment.

HOW GOD CALLS

Scripture shows us extensive examples of the *methods* God used to call men and women to his purposes. Understanding those methods will help us in our own discernment as women leaders.

In the Old Testament, God primarily called human beings by speaking directly to them. The long and distinguished list of Old Testament characters who heard God speak directly includes Noah, Abraham, Moses, Aaron, Joshua, David, Solomon, and almost every prophet.

While the Bible alternately describes God's voice as thunderous (2 Samuel 22:14), mighty (Psalm 68:33), and still or small (1 Kings 19:12, NKJV), we do not know exactly how it sounded to humans. In most cases, God's voice was clear to the intended recipient, but we do not know whether it would have been understandable or even audible to anyone else in the vicinity. The story of God's calling of Samuel indicates that the young boy heard an audible voice and assumed that Eli was calling to him. Eli did not hear the voice but soon recognized that Samuel was hearing the voice of the Lord.

In addition to speaking directly, God sometimes also utilized signs and wonders, divine messengers or angels, or dreams and visions to communicate his direction. For example, God spoke to Moses through a burning bush (Exodus 3:1-3); sent messengers to Abraham and Sarah (Genesis 18:1-15), Jacob (Genesis 32:24), Moses (Exodus 3:4), and Gideon (Judges 6:11-12); and communicated to Abraham, Jacob, Joseph, Solomon, and many prophets via dreams (Genesis 15:1).[2]

In the Old Testament, God also spoke through other human beings. Prophets frequently gave people instruction on God's behalf and provided divine interpretation of dreams. And Esther's uncle Mordecai persuaded the queen to speak to King Xerxes on behalf of her Jewish people, pointing out her privileged position and opportunity: "Who knows but that you have come to your royal position for such a time as this?" (Esther 4:14).

In the New Testament, God's method of calling people took an additional form. In the Gospels, Jesus could still issue in-person invitations and instructions, such as when he called his disciples and later sent out the twelve and then the seventy (Luke 9–10). The New Testament also describes several stories of believers receiving direction through visions: Ananias was instructed to meet the newly converted Saul (Acts 9:10-11); Peter was told that the gospel was meant for Gentiles and Jews alike (Acts 10:9-16); and Paul received an invitation from a "man of Macedonia" and concluded that it was the Lord's direction (Acts 16:9-10).

By and large, however, the Holy Spirit became the primary means of communicating calling or direction to believers in the early church. Before his ascension, Jesus promised the Holy Spirit to his followers as a helper, comforter, teacher, and reminder of God's Word and presence (John 14:15-27). This promise was fulfilled initially at Pentecost (Acts 2:1-4), and from that point on, the apostles relied on the Spirit for direction and power in their ministry.

In Acts 13, the Holy Spirit instructed church leaders, "Set apart for me Barnabas and Saul [Paul] for the work to which I have called them" (verse 2). And just before Paul's vision of the man from Macedonia, the apostle and his companions were "kept by the Holy Spirit from preaching the word in the province of Asia" and prevented by the "Spirit of Jesus" from entering Bithynia (Acts 16:6-7).

Direction from the Holy Spirit was often coupled with human confirmation. For example, the council at Jerusalem sent Barnabas and Paul to Gentile believers in Antioch, Syria, and Cilicia, along with instructions that "seemed good to the Holy Spirit and to us" (Acts 15:22-35). Whenever I read the New Testament, I am struck by how much ongoing conversation with God—prayer—pervaded life in the early church. Time and again, we read of God responding to believers praying together, whether it was for discernment of next steps, deliverance from trials, or grace and growth for the body of Christ. The apostles continually listened for the Lord's direction as they spread the gospel and led the early church. And Paul exhorted the church at Thessalonica to "pray continually" and to "not quench the Spirit" (1 Thessalonians 5:17, 19).

Although God initiates calling, biblical examples show us

the importance of human conversation and cooperation in the calling process. God provides the calling, but he has also provided us with the ability to reason about, reflect on, and respond to that calling.

THE PROCESS OF CALLING

While the actual calling of a person in the Bible is usually described (or read) as a singular event, that event was just one point in a greater process. Moses spent forty years of preparation in the desert before God called him to lead the Israelites out of Egypt. David served as a shepherd and a soldier between being anointed as the future king of Israel and actually ascending to the throne. Esther served King Xerxes faithfully for five years before she had the opportunity to ask his mercy for the Jewish people. Jesus spent three years preparing his disciples for their eventual commission.

The specific calling also demanded a response. Many chose to respond immediately in submission and obedience. Others, such as Moses, resisted for a time before finally acquiescing. Some chose, at times, to take matters into their own hands, due to lack of faith. Although God promised Abraham that he would have many descendants, Abraham and Sarah grew impatient with God's timetable and arranged for Abraham to sleep with Hagar, Sarah's slave (Genesis 16:1-3). And then there was Jonah, who was instructed to go to Nineveh and instead decided to flee in the opposite direction, toward Tarshish (Jonah 1:1-3).

The biblical pattern to the process of calling—preparation, discernment, and response—also applies to believers today.

As we examine each part of this process in greater detail, think about how a greater understanding of the general process may illuminate specific points on your own calling journey.

Preparation

The duration and focus of the season of preparation are different for each person. Preparation for a calling may take weeks, months, or years. God may develop our awareness, our understanding, our compassion, our character, our knowledge, our tangible skills. According to author and professor J. Robert Clinton, the leadership-development process includes both "inner-life growth processes" to develop character and responsiveness to God's voice and "ministry maturing processes" to develop ministry and relationship competence.[3]

And as we go through this development, we may or may not be aware that God is preparing us for a future calling. For example, as a young mother, Kris had no idea that a seemingly random part-time job would equip her to fulfill a call to foster parenting ten years later:

> When my middle son was an infant, I was in a small group with a pediatric psychiatrist. Out of the blue, she asked me if I wanted a job two days a week as a receptionist in her office. Little did I know that this position would help train me on some of the ins and outs of Medicaid, teach me about First Steps, and bring me in close contact with many foster parents and their kiddos with high medical need. All of those

experiences were prepping me for my role as foster
and then adoptive mom to our medical-needs son.
I never saw that coming, but fortunately, God did.

Whether or not you are aware that you are in a particular
season of preparation, you can be assured of two truths: First,
God is always at work. And second, God never wastes anything. You may not be able to see the big picture, but God
does. He is always working in us "to will and to act in order
to fulfill his good purpose" (Philippians 2:13).

But this season of preparation can be a two-way street. As
God prepares us, we can ready ourselves for his calling. The
best place to start is by developing a posture of submission.

Jennie Allen writes, "99 percent of being in the will
of God is being wholly willing to be in the will of God."[4]
Claude Hickman reminds us, "We cannot expect to get
all the detailed instructions before we are willing to begin
walking the path."[5] In addition to developing this attitude
of submission, are you being obedient to your general calling to follow Christ, to your corporate calling as a member
of the body of Christ, and to your existing commitments
and responsibilities? The discovery of any extraordinary calling begins with ordinary obedience to what God has already
revealed.

In this time of preparation, we can also cultivate a listening ear for the Lord's voice. The term *discern* derives from
the Latin root for *discriminate*.[6] If we want to discern God's
calling, we must learn to discriminate between his voice and
the many others vying for our attention.

"I've identified three major voices in my life," explained

Jana, a nomadic folk musician and minister. "There's my voice, there's the voice of others, and there's God's voice. The more I hear his voice, the more I can discern between mine and others and his. It's just tuning your ear."

The best way to tune our ears is to regularly take time to listen to God's voice. There is just no substitute for unhurried, undistracted time in God's presence. Cherie, an author and speaker who helps couples work through money issues, explained how she approaches this kind of preparation: "I'm always going to put myself in the path of God: college chapel, church, listening to worship music, reading theologians and artists, mentors, prayer, Scripture," she said. "I want to up my exposure to God in unexpected places as well as in expected places."

"Taking time to get ready is . . . not an annoying interlude but an essential ingredient and part of his equipping," Ken Costa reminds us.[7] While God's calling does not rest on our readiness, our participation in the preparation process softens our hearts and our wills, making us receptive to better discern God's calling.

Discernment

The actual discernment of a specific calling often overlaps with the season of preparation. Like preparation, discernment is often a process that takes place over time. The process may begin with us asking God what he has for our lives. Often, however, the calling finds us, regardless of whether we have been actively looking for it.

I have talked with Christians who have been afraid of missing God's calling for their lives. From their perspectives, God's direction for their lives is a tightrope that is hard to see and even harder to walk. But I believe that if we are being obedient to what we already know and are communicating regularly with God, his will (which includes our calling) is more like the Grand Canyon: easy to see and hard to fall *out* of.[8]

Claude Hickman makes a helpful distinction between a map and a compass in the process of seeking God's direction. While our tendency is to want a map that will give us specific instructions, Hickman points out that a compass is actually more helpful:

> In the journey God will often lead you where there are no roads. . . .
>
> The only way to find our destination in the big picture of what God is doing is to live our lives by the direction of the compass. . . . The compass points the right direction and helps us determine the wrong maps from the ones God has purposed for us.[9]

And yet once our compass is set to True North, we will find that God also directs our specific steps. God does not play some kind of cosmic hide-and-seek. Jesus promised, "Ask and it will be given to you; seek and you will find; knock and the door will be opened to you. For everyone who asks receives; the one who seeks finds; and to the one who knocks, the door will be opened" (Matthew 7:7-8).

Your process of discerning God's calling will look different from anyone else's. It may be different from what you thought it would (or should) look like. Be open to whatever means God chooses to use for you. "Our heavenly Guide does not deal with us *en masse*, but has personal and individual transactions with each," J. Oswald Sanders points out. "Since each of us is unique, He employs as many methods as there are people."[10]

Elizabeth, a missionary who works with a human-trafficking-prevention ministry, affirmed this truth: "God created me the way he created me, and he knows how he created me. When he calls me, he knows how I need to work through that. Whatever my calling, God's going to take me through it in the way he knows I need to go through it."

God may use a different method than you expected, but you can trust that he knows the right method for you. Every calling ultimately originates from God, and he can use both supernatural and natural means to communicate that call.[11]

SUPERNATURAL MEANS

According to Elisabeth Elliot, supernatural methods of calling can include visible or audible signs, angels, dreams and visions, and prophets.[12] While these means are less familiar to many of us today, God can and still does use them, and we must be open to the possibility of this type of communication regarding our calling.

Dorothy received a call to pastoral ministry through visible and audible signs. Dorothy had been teaching about the Bible on weekend nights at her local city hall, which was on a street filled with clubs. Her ministry was bearing much fruit in the form of conversions, but she discovered that local churches were not equipped or even willing to accept these rough, new converts in their congregations.

"One day, [as I was] just driving down the street," she

recalled, "a butt print appeared on the seat next to me. I was not afraid. I looked at it in amazement, and I heard an audible voice say, 'You are having babies and you are putting them in foster homes.' I cried my eyes out, went home, and told my husband that I would have to pastor a church for these folks. He said, 'I know; I've been waiting on you to realize it.'"

Dorothy is not the only woman to have experienced this kind of supernatural element to her calling. Others have described to me similar audible voices or visual signs. Some received a clear calling through a dream or a vision—a sense of dreaming while awake. A few reported receiving what they felt was prophetic direction from a third party, someone who would not have known their situation without divine mediation. Supernatural means of calling are every bit as valid today as they were during Bible times. As with any method of calling, however, we must "test the spirits" to confirm that this communication is truly of God (1 John 4:1).

NATURAL MEANS

God can communicate a calling through any number of natural means—including duty, God's Word, prayer, human agents, gifts, experiences, desires and passions, and circumstances.[13] As we examine each of these methods, reflect on their role in your own life and calling journey. How might God be speaking to you right now?

- **Duty.** The most obvious natural means of calling—and indeed, our first step in following our specific calling— are our existing responsibilities. "'Do the next thing' is one of the best pieces of advice I have ever had," Elisabeth Elliot writes. "It works in any kind of situation, and is especially helpful when we don't know what to do. What if we don't even know what the 'next thing' is? We can find something. Some duty lies on our doorstep. The rule is Do It. The doing of that thing may open our eyes to the next."[14] As we faithfully fulfill our duties, we can seek God's further direction regarding a specific calling. These responsibilities might include marriage, parenting, aging parents, church or community commitments, or even household duties such as repairs, gardening, or meal preparation.

- **Human Agents.** God often uses human agents in our calling process, including parents, siblings, a spouse, children, friends, extended family, and even distant acquaintances. They may serve in a variety of ways: by providing an invitation that helps initiate or confirm a calling; by affirming a sense of calling or giftedness; by asking questions that provide clarity or additional direction; or by cautioning against a particular path.

  Historically, the wisdom of one's faith community has been a critical part of the calling process.[15] Only in recent church history have Christians taken a more individual approach to the calling-discernment process. "Dialogue stimulates thought and broadens vision," notes J. Oswald Sanders.[16] As King Solomon advises, "Listen to counsel and receive instruction, that you may be wise in your latter days" (Proverbs 19:20, NKJV).

WOMEN SPEAK:
EXPERIENCING GOD'S VOICE

How Do You Experience God's Voice or Direction?

- "For me, it's a burning desire or passion that won't go away."—*Carmille*

- "It's just a consistent word in my own spirit, something that I feel I need to do, or a person that comes to mind repeatedly, something that I can't let go. It's definitely a very quiet thing. It's not like Mary with an angel in front of her or a prophet telling me I'm going to be king."—*Amy*

- "He speaks to me individually, but it's confirmed everywhere: worship music, reading Scripture, radio spots, sermons, prayer, people telling me things. Everywhere I turn, God brings me back to this thing that he's pointed out."—*Jes*

- "I 'hear' God's voice through journal prayers. I write something, then I write what I feel God's response is. I'm not sure how this works, but I am often surprised at God's response, like they're not actually my own thoughts but just flowing out of my pen."—*Tammi*

- "When I was called into youth ministry, I had a true epiphany moment. I heard someone talking about going into ministry and suddenly the world froze and my ears started ringing. I heard a voice say, 'You!'"—*Allison*

- "God speaks to me through how others see God moving in me and through me. I'm always looking for what is reflected back from my community, the people who know me best."—*Juliet*

Caroline is a pastor in a denomination with a lengthy confirmation process for prospective ministers. "I find a huge sense of confidence in the process I've gone through with ordination, and the affirmation I've received from church leadership and from presbytery committees," she explained. "It's like, 'Yeah, I believe I'm called here, and so do a lot of other people.'"

While God can and does use people in the calling process, I must note a few important cautions. First, any human invitation must be checked and confirmed through prayer and Scripture. "Our gifts and destiny do not lie expressly in our parents' wishes, our boss's plans, our peer group's pressures, our generation's prospects, or our society's demands," writes Os Guinness.[17] In my church, we sometimes joke about people being "volun-told" for a ministry role, but underneath the humor, we firmly acknowledge that calling ultimately comes from God, not another human being.

Second, while it is wise to seek the input of others during the calling process, not all counsel should be accorded equal weight. Always seek guidance from mature believers who truly want God's best for you and who are as interested in listening as they are in talking. Make sure your friends are true friends who will ask hard questions, not just fans or followers who will say what you want to hear. Be wary of well-meaning family members who may be driven more by their own fears or interests. Don't be like the Old Testament king Ahab, who consulted only the prophets (four hundred of them!) he was sure would approve his desired course (1 Kings 22:1-40).

At the same time, remember that God may use *you* to clarify, confirm, or encourage someone *else's* calling. After a long season of discernment, Kate and her husband had answered God's calling to serve as foster parents. A few months later, Kate was shopping at a home-improvement store and struck up a conversation with a salesperson in the kitchen-countertop department:

> I just happened to mention fostering. She stopped me in my tracks and said, "Wait. Tell me more about that. I was just praying this morning for God to show me what is next for me. I am a new empty nester, and I have more time on my hands now. This is what I am supposed to do."
>
> By the time I left, we had exchanged information and she was making the call *that day* to sign up for foster-parent training.

If you sense the Spirit's nudging regarding someone else's calling, don't be afraid to speak the words God has given you. Several times, I have simply shared my own story or made a seemingly offhanded suggestion to a student, only to have them look at me like they had been struck by lightning because God had used my words to direct or confirm a calling. Even an unintentional comment may encourage another.

- **Gifts.** The Holy Spirit endows each believer with spiritual gifts for building up the body of Christ (Romans 12:6-8; 1 Corinthians 12:4-11; Ephesians 4:11-16;

1 Peter 4:10). These might include teaching, leading, prophesying, helping, or administrating, among many others; the lists in the Bible are not necessarily exhaustive, and there may be as many unique gifts as there are believers.

God often calls people to roles that fit their gifts. Gifting is not an automatic indication of calling, however. As Carmille Akande writes, "Just because we have these gifts doesn't mean God is calling us to use them at *every* opportunity. We still must ask ourselves, 'Is this the will of God for my life?'"[18]

God can call the gifted, but he can also gift those he has called. He can even issue a calling out of our weakness or failure. A contemporary corporate-consulting firm would never have recommended the men Jesus chose as his disciples. The Bible is full of similar examples of God using the least qualified candidates for his Kingdom work—a fact that should give all of us great hope!

- **Experiences.** Our life experiences can serve to guide and shape our calling. We may experience success at a particular pursuit and, in that success, discover a passion that in turn becomes a calling. We may discover our calling in the process of simply responding to the needs around us. Or we may look back and see a recurring theme in our personal history and realize evidence of a "progressive calling" from God.[19]

From a very early age, Janette remembered three recurring themes in her life: teaching, leadership, and pastoral ministry. "When I was a little kid, I would teach my toys and stuffed animals," she recalled. As she grew older, Janette found herself in leadership roles. "When I went to high school, I found myself just leading things. I didn't even know why," she related. "The juniors and seniors asked me to help them start a Christian club. Then the juniors became seniors, and then they graduated." Janette kept leading and teaching. "We were packing my home. I don't even know how they got to my house!"

Meanwhile, Janette realized she loved the church. "I just loved pastoral ministry," she said. "I loved being at church, and I loved any church I was part of." Those three themes converged in a calling to bridge the church and academia, a calling Janette fulfills today through dual roles as pastor and seminary professor.

God can also grow our calling from negative experiences, bringing beauty from the ashes of past sin or failure. Jennifer's story is a powerful illustration of God's ability to redeem any experience for our calling and his glory:

After living fifteen years as a meth addict, enslaved to men, held captive by the pain of a past that included several abortions, I answered God's call to know Jesus as my Savior, and he delivered me from my addiction. I became involved with Celebrate Recovery, which was a healing and growing place for me as God started revealing to me my strengths in teaching and counseling.

At an orientation for a faith-based education program for addiction counselors, a professor said, "God uses our past for his purpose." He shared the great need for Christian counselors who have a recovery background. As he spoke, my heart leapt with excitement and joy, and the hair on my arms stood up. It felt as if God had touched my spirit and confirmed the purpose that I had been created for. Since then, God has opened up countless opportunities to facilitate his healing in the lives of numerous women of all ages and backgrounds.

Remember, God never wastes anything. Even if our experiences do not directly translate to our calling, they become part of our story and shape who we are, which in turn shapes how we live out our calling.

- **Desires and Passions.** When properly checked, our personal desires and passions—the things we emotionally value—can be a legitimate indicator of calling. Our feelings are a central part of our humanity and reflect the image of God. The Bible tells us that Jesus wept over the death of his friend Lazarus (John 11:1-44) and over the city of Jerusalem (Luke 19:28-41). Similarly, God can place a burden on our hearts for a particular people group or type of ministry. I have a heart for ministry leaders. My friend Hayley has a passion for underprivileged minorities. Other friends minister out of a burden for orphans, women, business executives, Native Americans, the homeless, and the unevangelized in Africa.

Ben Campbell Johnson argues that our emotions are a critical component of our calling: "Until the call becomes part of us emotionally, it is nothing more than a notion in our heads that we can manipulate and control. Attaching feelings to our images incarnates the call in our flesh-and-blood story, and passion begins to drive it."[20]

At the same time, our feelings can be fickle. God has created us as emotional beings, yet our emotions may reflect flawed understanding. They are a gauge, not a guide.[21] What, then, *should* be the proper place for our emotions, passions, or desires in the calling process?

Each of us has a particular bent for or against emotion. As women, the likelihood is that many of us (although certainly not all, myself included) skew toward the emotional side. I suggest that as we seek to discern our calling, we make room for whichever side falls opposite of our default approach. God can certainly use our passions to guide us, but those passions must be tempered by objective truth. At the same time, God can guide us through our thoughts, but our minds must remain open to emotion and the possibility of mystery in the calling journey.

In addition, the more closely and regularly we walk with God, the more our desires will align with his desires. Our hearts will instruct our minds, and our minds will instruct our hearts (Psalm 16:7; Colossians 3:1-2). We will not need to fear—or hide in—either emotion or reason.

- **Circumstances.** Circumstances are literally those things that happen around us.[22] They are the easiest of all the natural means to detect and are therefore a commonly used measure of God's direction. Certainly, there are times when God uses circumstances or seemingly random occurrences to initiate, direct, or confirm our calling. An open door or closed door. A passage from a book. A sermon from the pulpit or on the radio. A timely worship song.

  We can all point to instances where circumstances helped confirm direction from God. We even see an example of this in the Bible, when Gideon famously tested God by putting out a fleece and asking him to perform miracles to prove his presence (Judges 6:36-40).

  We must be very careful about assigning meaning to an event, however. Ease of observation does not guarantee accuracy of interpretation. We could be looking only for what we *want* to see. An open door could be a sign of God's favor, or it could be a spiritual test. An obstacle in our path could be a signal to turn around and go in a different direction, or it could be a challenge to overcome.

  "In decisions of far-reaching importance, especially, circumstances should play a minor part. Coincidence never negates God's command," counsels J. Oswald Sanders.[23] Circumstances must be checked against the truths of Scripture and confirmed by the conviction of the Holy Spirit.

- **God's Word.** The Bible serves as a plumb line against which to evaluate any perceived calling by other means.

While personal emotions, passions, and desires can be used to discern God's calling, these must be tested in light of the unchanging truths of God's Word. And as J. Oswald Sanders tells us, "Where Scripture speaks clearly, no further guidance need be sought."[24]

To know God's Word, we must spend regular time in it, "reading and studying the whole will of God as found in the whole Word of God."[25] God's Word is "a lamp to [our] feet and a light to [our] path" (Psalm 119:105, NASB); "alive and active" (Hebrews 4:12); illuminated by the Holy Spirit (John 16:12-15; 1 Corinthians 2:6-16); and will never return empty (Isaiah 55:11). When we seek to discern God's calling, we must spend time in Scripture.

- **Prayer.** Direction *from* God requires dialogue *with* God. Elizabeth Liebert writes that "a life of personal and corporate prayer is the single most important preparation for discernment."[26]

  Like any true dialogue, prayer should include not only telling and asking but also listening. Listen for what God may want to say to you, but also listen to yourself. Beth Booram writes:

  > Pay attention to what you are praying. Not the rote or dispassionate prayers, but the ones that have a quality of unbiddenness. Prayers that overtake you. Prayers that you can't "not" pray. They form in you . . . from the swirl of desire and desperation merging together, giving voice to your deep yearning. Those

prayers can indicate where God is preparing to or has implanted the seed of a dream.[27]

As with time in God's Word, time spent in prayer is absolutely essential—"obvious wisdom"[28]—to discern our God-given calling. Prayer forces us to slow down, evaluate our hearts, and consider God's perspective.

"In prayer, as I sit and wait, pressing into his presence, I receive strong impressions in my spirit, like heavenly vibes, that influence me," explained Jennifer, a minister and alcohol-and-addictions counselor.

Janette, a seminary professor and pastor, practices the Prayer of Examen—a prayerful review of her day[29]—as a method of regular communication with God. "The Prayer of Examen has been helpful to show me where I was able to give the most love, or the least; where I felt the most grace, the most life-giving moments," Janette said. "Those kinds of movements over the years have illuminated some of the choices I made."

Regardless of the form your prayers take, commit to making regular time for conversation with God as a means of discerning, confirming, and directing your calling.

Response

Once we have received an invitation or direction from God, we must choose whether and how to respond. As Ben Campbell Johnson points out, "All efforts to listen to the call of God, to scan our memories for clues, to look for signs of God's presence, to engage in the struggles with God and

WOMEN SPEAK: DIVINE REDIRECTION

In what ways have you had to fundamentally change your life in order to obey your calling?

- "All of it: specifically, giving up my home, my possessions, and my place to become available and open to going when and where called."—*Jana*

- "Maybe not the answer you'd expect, but God has called me to rest for many years. As I am learning to obey that call, I'm having to give up time in a different way. Rather than giving up my time in order to 'do,' he asks me to give up 'doing' in order to give him my time and to 'be.'"—*Jes*

- "We moved across the country, just two weeks married, to a place where we knew no one. That changed everything."—*Tammi*

- "I was a CPA with much higher earning potential. When I was called into ministry, I gave up the money, the status, so many worldly things. And I don't regret it at all."—*Nicole*

- "When God called me to be a pastor and relocate, it also meant letting go of the 'things' that I relied on for substance in my life. Going from a house of 3,500 square feet to 1,350 square feet with not one of my family's treasures was a time of deep grieving, but it was also very liberating. I discovered that I already had an inheritance, a priceless treasure."—*Jennifer*

ourselves, and to listen to the reflections of others—all these efforts are wasted unless we act."[30]

The first response required is actually one of the heart, not of our hands or feet. As leaders, it may be tempting to rush into action. But the central issue is whether we will surrender to God. The discovery of our callings is a divine disruption that requires us to make a choice beyond mere intellectual assent. Will we keep doing what we have been doing, or will we fundamentally reorient our lives so that we can join God's work? The more closely we have walked with God through the preparation and discernment phases of the calling process, the better prepared our hearts will be to respond in submission.

Make no bones about it: Surrender costs us everything. "We hand over every dream for our lives—every hope, every remnant of control we think we have—to God, and we say, 'You have all of it. You have me. I am yours. Anything you want to do with me. Anything. I am in,'" writes Jennie Allen.[31] Yet the death of our agenda is the only way to life in our calling. We all eventually surrender to something—or to someone. Will it be to God and the fullness he promises, or to our own illusions of control based on our limited perspectives?

We do not need to know all the details of a calling in order to begin obeying it. On the contrary, knowing every step is a hindrance to faith.[32] Tyler Blanski relates the following story about Mother Teresa's perspective on faith and calling:

A man who worked for three months at "the house of the dying" in Calcutta . . . was seeking a clear

answer about what God wanted him to do with his
life. He asked [Mother Teresa] to pray for him.

"What do you want me to pray for?" she asked.

"Pray that I would have clarity," he said.

"No, I will not do that," she said.

When he asked her why, she explained: "Clarity is
the last thing you are clinging to and must let go of."

When he mentioned that *she* always seemed to
have clarity, Mother Teresa just laughed: "I've never
had clarity; all I've ever had is trust. So I will pray
that you trust in God."[33]

But faith is not blind obedience, either. Ken Costa
explains: "It's more like leaving a house with a friend to go
on a journey. You both have a shared destination in mind
and a map to get you there, but there are many routes you
could take along the way. And so you work out your route
in conversation and relationship."[34]

When we are communicating with God regularly and
have surrendered our will to his, faith is not a leap; it's a
series of steps. All we have to do is the next thing. And that
next thing is often much simpler than we imagine. Instead
of looking for something grand, start by taking care of the
mundane, as Os Guinness reminds us:

We look for the big things to do—Jesus took a
towel and washed the disciples' feet. We presume
the place to be is the mountaintop of vision—he
sends us back into the valley. We like to speak and
act out of the rare moments of inspiration—he

requires our obedience in the routine, the unseen, and the thankless. Our idea for ourselves is the grand moment and the hushed crowd—his is ordinary things when the footlights are switched off.[35]

"I used to tie myself in knots, asking, *Is this God? Is this not God?*" confessed Carolyn, a fifty-year-old pastor. "I finally decided I am just going to take one step in the direction that I can best discern. I don't get hung up on what my calling is going to look like when it's fully lived out. That has really set me free because I'm such a control freak and planner."

Your next step may be a simple phone call. An email. Some online research. A yes instead of a no. Ten minutes of your time. A few of your dollars. More prayer. A lunch meeting. An exploratory trip. With each step we take, the next one becomes clearer. A life of leadership begins with the little things.

WHAT NOW?

As you enter into seasons of discernment about your calling, there are a few important things you must keep in mind.

First, *the calling process is mysterious.* God can use any method he chooses to issue a calling, and he can work outside any box in which you try to contain him. He can use both natural and supernatural means to communicate his purpose for your life. Just as there is no one-size-fits-all calling, the calling process is unique to each person.

But second—even amid the mystery, *calling is not secret.* You can pursue postures and practices to help you hear and discern God's voice and direction for your life. With God's help, you can develop a listening ear, an obedient heart, and ready hands and feet.

Third, as you seek your calling, *trust the process.* Be patient. Wait on the Lord. Seek him with all your heart. Look for him in expected and unexpected places. Allow him to mold you. Trust his goodness and his timing. He will guide you as you walk with him, step by step.

CONTINUE THE CONVERSATION

» Do you view God's will for you as more of a tightrope or a canyon?

» Is there an area where you have received *enough* direction to step out instead of waiting for more details?

» Do you know your Shepherd's voice? How does God make his voice clear to you? How are you cultivating a listening ear?

» As you look back, how has God prepared you for your current calling or season of life?

» Are you fully surrendered to God, or are you currently resisting him in any matter of your calling?

» What is the next thing you should do in regard to your calling?

Chapter 3

CALLING AND AUTHORITY

Oh boy, here we go. It's the chapter on authority.

I can already sense some of your hackles rising in antici-pation. Mention *authority* around women leaders, and the conversation can get charged in a hurry. Strong rhetoric emanates from organizations and individuals all laying claim to the "biblical" perspective.[1] There is no shortage of either opinion or emotion about this topic.

So what in the world am I going to say about calling and authority?

I bet it's not what you think.

There are plenty of books that address the question "Can a woman preach?" (or teach, or lead, or be a pastor). This is not one of them.

I've had a complex relationship with this topic of authority in my own leadership development journey. I grew up in a church that had male elders, pastors, and deacons, and female "ministry directors" and deaconesses. Although that church would have described itself as "complementarian" regarding gender roles (i.e., women were to submit to the authority of men in ministry and in the home), I don't recall hearing a sermon or other teaching at my church that specifically addressed the issue of gender and calling. In fact, the leaders there seemed very supportive of my decision to major in youth ministry in college. One of our pastors even asked me to start a youth ministry at a church he planted in a neighboring community.

At my Christian college, both men and women were affirmed as potential ministry leaders. I led freely as a worship leader in chapel, as a volunteer youth leader in several churches, and at a Christian camp during the summer. It wasn't until after college and into seminary, ministry, and doctoral studies that I began to realize there were other (very strong) perspectives on women in leadership and ministry. Those perspectives didn't really affect my ability to fulfill my calling, as I worked at a parachurch ministry and had no desire to be a pastor. They *did* affect my confidence and sense of self, however, as I began to question whether my leadership bent was a gift or a fatal feminine flaw. I asked God to help me be more meek and gentle. I tried to blend in, to not take charge; and yet, even when I went out of my way to *not* lead something, people usually ended up looking to me for clarity or direction.

Finally, after a long season of anguished prayer and reflection, I realized that the problem was not that I was a leader or a woman but that I was trying to deny who God had created me to be. I vividly remember the moment of clarity when I wrote in my journal: I AM A LEADER. From that day on, I committed to the Lord that I would not bury the gifts or calling he had given me.

I wish I could say it has been smooth sailing since then, but of course, my calling has also been impacted by human systems. There have been times when I have had to hold my tongue, and other times when I have felt compelled to speak up. I have been told by some that my calling is a blessing to the body of Christ and by others that by following it, I am disobeying God. I have felt frustration over lack of support or opportunity—and the pain and then freedom of moving to new systems. In the process, God's voice has become clearer, my conviction deeper, and my sense of calling stronger.

That's why, in this chapter, I want to *reframe* and *personalize* the issue of authority as it pertains to your leadership calling. I want to challenge you to rethink the whole idea of authority, and I want to help you consider how the concept of authority applies specifically to *you* in light of your God-given calling.

Because here's the thing: Your beliefs about this "authority" issue—whatever they are, whatever that word even means to you—are not a prerequisite for salvation, a test of orthodoxy, or a measure of commitment to justice.

Read that last sentence again, and again if needed, until your pulse returns to resting rate.

Some of you have been deeply wounded in the name of "authority." Hear me clearly: I do not mean to downplay those very real hurts. Others of you are concerned that certain perspectives on this issue compromise the very integrity, the *authority*, of God's Word. I applaud and share your desire to maintain a high view of Scripture.

These are important issues and reasons why the topic of authority is so emotionally charged. But I believe another reason it is so easy to get worked up about the issue of authority is that we tend to think of it primarily in terms of human permission, or *authorization*: Who can do what, and who gets to decide? The result is a battle for position on a ladder, with God presumably at the top but a lot of ugly jostling on the rungs below.

Permission is indeed one component of authority, and one that we will explore on a more personal level of application. But I want to reframe and expand the conversation by redefining authority not in terms of authorization but of *accountability*. Those who have been called have been entrusted with responsibility. Who should they be responsible to, and who are they responsible for?

AUTHORITY AND SCRIPTURE

While there are several levels to calling and various ways God can extend a leadership call, nowhere does the Bible teach that either gifts or secondary callings are bestowed according to gender. In fact, women preached, prophesied, and led in both the Old and New Testaments . . . sometimes over men. (See the examples of Deborah in Judges 4–5, Huldah in 2 Kings 22, Anna in Luke 2, Priscilla in Acts 18, and Junia in Romans 16.[2]) The *exercise* of calling was sometimes limited by gender, but the *fact* of calling was not.

The Bible is also clear that God is proauthority. Scripture describes authority systems in the home, church, government, and spiritual realms. Christ followers are commanded to honor those in authority, even as God claims ultimate authority over these individuals and systems (Romans 13:1).

The Bible also calls believers to accountability, even in the absence of human authority systems. Scripture clearly teaches that Christ followers are ultimately accountable to God for their thoughts, words, and actions. In addition, the Bible provides examples of accountability between human beings, not only to those in authority but also to colaborers and even those under someone's care. In the New Testament in particular, the twelve apostles and then the seventy-two disciples sent by Jesus gave a report of their ministry (Luke 9:10, 10:17); believers in the early church reported to the whole fellowship (Acts 15:4); and the apostles gave seven men responsibility to care for widows via the distribution of food (Acts 6:1-7).

The examples of accountability in Scripture proceed from the key biblical principles of *stewardship* and *community*. Throughout the Bible, we see the theme of stewardship. God entrusts human beings with relationships, wealth, material resources, power, time, truth, responsibility, spiritual gifts— and calling. Each person will be expected to give account of how they cared for (stewarded) their assigned responsibilities (Matthew 25:14-30). Throughout the Bible, we also see that the people of God are people of community. They worship together, serve together, and grow as they live in relationship together. The "one another" exhortations of the New Testament—there are more than thirty!—can only be fulfilled in the context of community.

In particular, this community is experienced and expressed through participation in a local church. The word *church* (the Greek *ekklēsia*) literally refers to God's gathered people, and those gatherings took place publicly, locally, and regularly. In the early church, an "unchurched Christian" would have been an oxymoron.

The concept of authority is important, but we need to understand it within the broader principle of accountability. The Gospel of Matthew records that during Jesus' teaching ministry on earth, he often answered questions about specific issues by saying, "You have heard it said, but I tell you . . ." His interlocutors wanted to pin him down on sticky issues and the letter of the law of Moses, but Jesus challenged his listeners to a higher standard based on the spirit of the law of love (Matthew 5:38-39).

In the same way, we can easily focus only on the permission question of "Can a woman teach/preach/lead?" and lose sight of the broader biblical theme of accountability and its related principles of community and stewardship. But these themes provide a necessary framework to help us determine how to faithfully live out our callings.

CALLING AND ACCOUNTABILITY

Authority is about having power *over*; accountability is about being responsible *to* and *for*. "Being responsible" requires a measure of submissiveness regardless of gender, age, experience, or position. Accountability is clearly a theme in the Bible. The important question is not whether Christians should be accountable but to whom. The first, most obvious answer is God, but that is not the only answer.

As we see throughout Scripture, Christians are also accountable to other humans. These could include people in authority (such as an employer or supervisor), people who are impacted by close relationship (such as a spouse, coworker, or even an employee or a congregant), and people who have been voluntarily enlisted to provide personal accountability (such as a friend or mentor).

Leaders are *never* exempt from this human accountability, no matter their title or type of Kingdom service. As Paul writes in 1 Corinthians 12, all Christians are equal and essential members of the body of Christ. While some may serve in oversight positions, leaders should not separate themselves from the body, whether in thought or in practice. To think that a person is accountable only to God creates the dangerous situation of a person believing they are above all other people, which results in abuses of position and power.

The opposite danger is to think that a person is accountable only to other humans. This path leads to fear and vacillating behavior based on human fickleness. But godly leaders in any type of ministry must be willing to make unpopular decisions. As Paul questions, "Am I now trying to win the approval of human beings, or of God? Or am I trying to please people? If I were still trying to please people, I would not be a servant of Christ" (Galatians 1:10).

Although we are accountable to both God and humans, it is crucial for us to have the right parties on the list and to keep them in the right priority: God first, then the people closest to us and most impacted by our actions, then others. "Pick your voices and then be prepared and willing to disappoint the rest," writes Jennie Allen. "We have to decide whom we will listen to and whom we won't. You are not obligated to bend to the convictions and judgment of every person around you, or you will never do anything. Choose to obligate yourself to a few trusted voices."[4]

For Allen, that means, "Scripture. The Holy Spirit. My husband. My elders and mentor. My small group of friends who love God deeply and aren't afraid to kick me in the tail or push me to obey, even if my obedience looks different from theirs. To these voices I submit; I receive truth and I count the cost."[5]

Jessica, a twenty-seven-year-old seminary student, has chosen to develop a personal Board of Directors to serve as a sounding board and accountability team. "There are about seven or eight people," she explained. "They are all from different life stages, some men, some women, some married, others are single, some are parents, some are not. A lot of them have played impactful roles in different seasons in my life.

"Board of Directors sounds so 'CEO-esque' but I have invited them to speak into my life in this mentor-y role," Jessica continued. "I tell them, 'Push me. Speak into my life. Ask hard questions.' They are 'my people,' and I have invited them into this ongoing conversation. I usually talk to them once a month, just to check in. I also emailed them about whether to move to Salt Lake City [a few years ago], and I talked to them when I was deciding whether to go to seminary."

WOMEN SPEAK:
ACCOUNTABILITY

To whom (besides God) are you accountable as you pursue your calling?

- "My husband, my department head (who is also a teaching pastor at our church), my life group, my women's leadership team, and my closest friends."—*Pauline*

- "No one. Maybe that's the problem . . ."—*Jes*

- "Those who would be affected by my obedience to my calling."—*Jessica*

- "Those who I am called to serve."—*Amy*

- "My family. My husband reminds me that my relationship with God comes first, but my family comes second. Ministry can be a close third. If I lead others well in my calling but neglect the precious ones God has specifically given me to raise, I have failed."—*Cortney*

- "My husband and I pray together and talk things over with each other, but then we also lean into mentors. We share what's happening in our hearts and on our journeys, and we give them full permission to speak into our lives."—*Sherry*

Kelly, a thirty-seven-year-old writer, has found accountability with her husband, with her editors, with her church's leadership, and in a "mastermind group" with two other women. "The mastermind group has been such a blessing," she said. "Since I've 'gone out on my own' as a writer, I miss the accountability of being on a ministry team. The mastermind group is my sounding board, cheerleading section, prayer team, and accountability partner, keeping me on course with deadlines and about which projects I take."

Every female leader needs to determine to whom (besides God) they are accountable. Some of these people might be assumed or easy to identify, such as a supervisor. But beyond those in positional authority, which people in your life are impacted by your decisions? A spouse? Children? Extended family? Friends or colleagues? Then, beyond those impacted by your actions: To whom will you voluntarily give permission—*authority*—to speak into your life regarding the exercise of your calling?

CALLING AND STEWARDSHIP

After determining *to whom* a Christian should be accountable, the second important question is *for what* is a Christian accountable? In a word: everything. Romans 14:12 states that every believer will give account of themselves to God. This includes behaviors, beliefs, attitudes, and anything else for which they were given responsibility. This is *stewardship*. Again, leaders are not exempt from this responsibility. As Andy Stanley points out: "Leadership is a stewardship. It's temporary, and you're accountable."[6]

From the foundations of the universe (Genesis 1), God entrusted human beings with care of his creation and everything that flows from it. As we have seen in Scripture, that includes all manner of relationships and resources: Our marriages. Our kids. Our health. Our wealth. Our possessions. Our friendships. Our jobs. Our influence. And . . . our callings.

Did you catch that? We are responsible to God for any calling that he has extended to us.

I'm a pastor's wife, and people at our church sometimes ask me for information about various ministry programs, policies, and procedures. Many times, I do not know the answer, so my standard explanation (delivered with a wink) is, "The less I know, the less I am responsible for." Of course, I am joking about my role as a pastor's wife. But there is a sense that if I know something, I am responsible for what I do with that information. And if I have heard a calling from God, whether general or specific, I am responsible for what I do with it.

"God is not at all concerned with the number of books I sell or the size of my readership," said Tricia, a forty-year-old author. "He is concerned with how I will steward my influence. I must keep this in mind when I am in meetings with editors and publishers who long for greatness, who have giant visions for what my writing will do and become. It may happen; it may not. But I am committed to being faithful to the God who lit the flame in the first place. He will do what he will do. I will be faithful to him and to the practice."

If you have received a calling, you are a steward of that calling. Will you ignore it, deny it, muffle it, or follow it? How will you steward that calling in accountability to God and to the people he has called you to serve?

CALLING AND COMMUNITY

While Christians are ultimately accountable to God for their calling, the biblical principle of community—of living in close relationship with our brothers and sisters in Christ—influences both the process and the practice of that calling.

Community and the Process of Calling

Throughout church history, a person's calling has been affirmed in the context of community, specifically within a local church. A number of church denominations still utilize a "mutual calling" process when hiring pastoral staff: Not only must a potential minister sense an "internal call" to the pastorate but a congregation must discern and issue an "external call" affirming the candidate's calling, preparation, and readiness for ministry.[7]

But this communal affirmation process does not need to be restricted to prospective clergy. Given the Bible's emphasis on community, the faith community should play a critical role in *any* individual's calling-discernment process.

"In communal affirmation, there is what theologian and scholar Dr. Phil Collins called a 'check and balance' of the mutual submission for our callings," writes Sarah Bessey. "The people of God recognize and discern the gift; the individual then discerns, responds, and submits; then after the commissioning, the community receives the practice within the church and in the world."[8]

The Religious Society of Friends, also known as the Quakers, practice a "clearness committee" that serves this purpose. The individual seeking discernment "meets with three or four other Friends," who sit together "in a spirit of worship, listening and loving concern."[9] The committee listens deeply, gently asking open-ended questions and reflecting back what they have heard from the individual and the Holy Spirit regarding the issue at hand.

Of course, a process like this requires that a person be engaged in a community of believers. And if we are to take biblical teachings and examples seriously, that community should be found in the context of a local church. Unfortunately, commitment to this type of community continues to decline.[10] Os Guinness laments, "One of the most bizarre features of the Western church is the incidence of Christian leaders who are undisciplined about regular worship in the assembly of God's people."[11] It is only in the last few centuries that Christians began to believe that spiritual growth could be achieved apart from a relationship with the church, which is the body and bride of Christ. This is a sad departure from Scripture—and nearly two millenia of church history across all theological persuasions.

Equally problematic is the fact that few churches have intentional pathways or programs to help non-clergy wrestle with the general concept of calling or their specific role in God's work. But these hurdles do not negate the fact that the process of weighing a calling cannot be a solo activity. We as women leaders must plant deep roots in community—specifically, in a local fellowship of believers—as part of the process of discovering our personal calling and of helping others do the same. This community can pray for us, ask discerning questions, share their observations of our lives and ministry, seek God's direction on our behalf, and speak truth into our lives.

You may need to help create this type of community. Risk reaching out: Greet someone new on Sunday. Invite someone

THE ONE ANOTHERS

Are you practicing these "one anothers"[3] in your own life?

- Be at peace with one another (Mark 9:50).
- Be of the same mind as one another (Romans 15:5).
- Accept one another (Romans 15:7, 14).
- Be kind, tenderhearted, and forgiving to one another (Ephesians 4:32).
- Bear with and forgive one another (Colossians 3:13).
- Love one another (John 13:34-35 and throughout the New Testament).
- Serve one another (Galatians 5:13; Philippians 2:3; 1 Peter 4:9, 5:5).
- Strengthen one another (Romans 14:19).
- Help one another (Hebrews 3:13, 10:24).
- Submit to one another (Ephesians 5:21; 1 Peter 5:5).
- Consider one another more important than yourselves (Philippians 2:3).
- Commit to one another (1 John 3:16).
- Bear one another's burdens (Galatians 6:2).
- Speak truth to one another (Ephesians 4:25).
- Do not lie to one another (Colossians 3:9).

to coffee. Share your story, and listen to theirs. Even small investments in relationships can bring rich rewards.

In the past, I have practiced individualism as much as anyone. Some of my previous churches did not recognize or affirm my gifts or calling in the first place, and others did not

- Pray for one another (James 5:16).
- Forgive one another (Colossians 3:13).
- Be devoted to one another (Romans 12:10).
- Be patient with one another (Ephesians 4:2; Colossians 3:13).
- Encourage one another (Romans 14:19; 15:14; Colossians 3:16; 1 Thessalonians 4:18; 1 Thessalonians 5:11; Hebrews 3:13; 10:24-25).
- Be accountable to one another (Ephesians 5:21).
- Confess sins to one another (James 5:16).
- Do not provoke or envy one another (Galatians 5:26).
- Have equal concern for one another (1 Corinthians 12:25).
- Speak to one another with psalms, hymns, and spiritual songs (Ephesians 5:19).
- Offer hospitality to one another without grumbling (1 Peter 4:9).
- Care for one another (Galatians 6:2).
- Do not slander one another (James 4:11).
- Be concerned for one another (Hebrews 10:24).

practice or encourage the process of exploration of calling in community. I am thankful I now belong to a faith community that allows and encourages me to explore and exercise my calling . . . which brings us to our next issue: the relationship of community to the *practice* of calling.

Community and the Practice of Calling

The actual practice of calling is where we get into the "permission" issue, or what we typically think of when we hear the word *authority* in relationship to calling.

Before we go further, let me issue a gentle reminder that there are godly men and women on both sides of the "authority/permission" issue regarding a woman's practice of her calling. They have reached their conclusions after much study, consideration, and prayer. Let's graciously listen to and respect our brothers' and sisters' convictions in this area.

The reality is that the practice of calling takes place in the context of human systems such as a family, a group, a church, a nonprofit organization, or a government entity. Each of those systems contains people who have been given positional authority to serve as the "gatekeepers" or permission givers for what is allowed in those systems. This is generally a good thing. As we saw earlier, God is not anti-authority, and Christians are to respect those placed in positions of authority. As long as everyone within the organization operates under the same assumptions, there is no conflict.

Tension arises when an individual's perspective does not line up with that of the permission givers. This tension may only be felt internally in the form of frustration and discouragement, or it may also manifest itself externally in the form of interpersonal conflict. Applied specifically to a woman's secondary calling, the permission issue will play out in one of two ways: either her calling is recognized, affirmed, and encouraged within her system, or there are restrictions placed on the recognition and/or practice of her calling within that system.

If you feel that you are in a system where your individual calling is recognized, affirmed, and released, I rejoice with you. What a gift! And if your perspective on women and calling lines up with that of your organization's leaders, that, too, is a gift.

If, however, you are a woman who has experienced a particular call on your life but do not feel affirmed or encouraged by those in authority in your system, you know all too well the tension of which I speak. You may find yourself questioning your gifts, your calling, and even your spiritual maturity and ability to hear the Lord. Jennie Allen recalls, "So many tensions lay on top of my calling because of my gender. I spent a bit of time wishing away my gender, but since that wasn't happening, I found myself wishing away my calling."[12]

In addition to questioning yourself, you may find yourself questioning the system: the perspective of those in authority, the fact of their authority, perhaps even their spiritual maturity and their ability to hear the Lord. And of course, there is the question of what a woman in this situation should do.

If you are in this dilemma, you have several options, each of which brings its own challenges:

- **Submit to Authority.** The first option is to subjugate your sense of calling to the authority of your system, either temporarily or long-term. On September 10, 1946, thirty-six-year-old Mother Teresa received what she termed a "call within a call" to serve Christ among the poorest of the poor.[13] Within a month, she shared this calling with her spiritual director.

> Mother Teresa wanted to act immediately upon her inspiration. Yet because she had consecrated her life to God through a vow of obedience, she could proceed only with the approval of her superiors. To her, their blessing was not a mere formality but a protection and assurance that God's hand was in the undertaking. Only their permission would give her the certainty that this call was indeed God's will and not some delusion.[14]

> Mother Teresa wrote to her superiors with increasing urgency over the next sixteen months, pleading for their permission to pursue what she felt was a God-given calling. Her obedience was an ongoing internal struggle. Finally, in January 1948, Archbishop Ferdinand Périer uttered the words she longed to hear: "You may go ahead."[15]

> Like Mother Teresa, you may feel it best to place yourself under the authority within your system, regardless of when—or even whether—permission might be granted for you to follow your calling. This choice of submission will both challenge and strengthen your patience and humility.

- **Proceed without Permission.** The second option is to prayerfully move ahead without permission—and perhaps even in the face of direct opposition—to your sense of calling. When asked pointedly whether he would recant his teachings, the great reformer Martin Luther declined, famously declaring, "Here I stand. I cannot do otherwise. God help me. Amen."[16] Luther felt he could not go against his own conscience as informed by the Word of God. Likewise, you might feel that your calling is truly something you "can't not do" and that you must break with those in authority in your system.

  When Jana and her husband felt called to leave their home and travel the United States with their two teenagers in a bus to minister as itinerant musicians, they heard numerous objections from family and friends. "They were saying, 'You guys are irresponsible,' 'You guys are crazy,' 'What are you doing to your kids?' 'You can't just live in a half-built bus with no plumbing and no electricity,'" Jana recalled. "We had no language to communicate it, but we just knew we were supposed to go."

  A choice like this may damage relationships with other human beings, even as you feel you are acting in obedience to God. However, such a weighty decision should never be made without serious prayer and consultation with mature believers, including men and women who are not directly involved in your situation.

- **Seek a New System.** The third option is to seek a new system entirely. If you feel that you are constantly hitting a ceiling, you may need to consider moving to a different context, which may mean a different organization, denomination, or community. This is the rationale that guided both Jenni and Fran to move to different ministry contexts.

"My calling to ministry certainly encountered obstacles in settings where other leaders genuinely didn't believe women could serve in certain roles," said Fran, who has served on staff at several churches. "It was my duty to be patient and pray in those situations. But it was also my duty to keep my eyes open for if and when the Lord wanted to move me on. I was called to be a minister, not a martyr."

Jenni explained her decision using the analogy of the best soil for a particular seed:

> One day, I was reading a devotional that said that part of our responsibility is to take the seed of the gift that God has given us and plant it in the soil that is best for that seed. I felt like God gave me the visual that I was not in the best soil to flourish. It wasn't bad soil—other seeds grow there—but it wasn't the right soil for me. I felt God's release to put that seed in different soil.

Like Fran and Jenni, you may sense God giving you permission to move to a new environment entirely. This is similar to the second option and sometimes accompanies the decision to move ahead without permission in another system. This can be a painful process, as it often involves loss of opportunity, relationships, and perhaps even paradigms of how you believed things were supposed to go. There are two primary challenges with this choice: one is to leave the old system graciously, and the other is to seek accountability in the new system.

These hard decisions take on even more weight given a leader's influence by example. Therefore, regardless of which options you consider, it is absolutely critical that you consult with wise counsel and cover the decision process with prayer. Our desires and emotions can quickly cloud our objectivity. Nevertheless, remember that even after much consideration and prayer, two parties seeking the same God and consulting the same Bible may come to different conclusions. There are times when Christians submit to one another and times when they agree to disagree and even to part ways (see Paul and Barnabas and, oh, the last two thousand years of church history).

WHAT NOW?

In my own journey of calling, I've walked this path in regard to authority: accountability and stewardship to the Lord and accountability to a group of people that includes my husband and mature Christians from inside and outside my current church. These friends support the fact of my personal calling but also challenge me regarding the best ways to fulfill it. But let's get personal: What does this idea of authority mean for *you* as you seek to follow God's calling?

First, understand that *God can call anyone to anything he chooses.* Without partiality, he calls men and women to follow him and to participate in his work in the world in any number of ways. One of the biggest hindrances to our calling is our own doubts about how we might work out that calling, which then cause us to question the calling itself. But: *You are a leader!* Accept and believe how God has called you, and don't allow yourself to doubt that call simply because of human systems.

Second, *submit to (and even seek) accountability.* You are ultimately accountable to God for the stewardship of your calling, but that does not exempt you from human accountability. Develop a network of people who have permission to speak into your life regarding the exercise of your calling.

Third, *commit to community.* Pursue deep relationships and put down roots in a local church. Involve this community as much as you can in both the process and the practice of your calling.

Finally, *remember that your calling is exercised within human systems.* Seek wisdom from the Lord and from your community about how and where to fulfill your calling. Remain humble and gracious even when there are differences of opinion.

CONTINUE THE CONVERSATION

» What has been your experience with "authority" in relation to your calling?

» What relationships and resources has God entrusted to your responsibility?

» To which human beings are you accountable as you pursue your calling? Do you need to add, delete, or change any names on that list?

» Are you currently living in intentional relationship in community—specifically, within a local church? If not, what changes do you need to make so that you are able to practice the "one anothers" of Scripture?

» Do you feel that your calling is affirmed and supported in your current faith community? If not, what seems to be your best option, based on prayer and wise counsel?

Chapter 4

CALLING AND MARRIAGE

We met in seminary. I was there following my call, and he was there following his. We found each other even though we weren't looking. Isn't that how love often works?

The relationship blossomed quickly. I blocked his jump shot in a pick-up basketball game on the seminary court, and we ended up talking long after everyone left . . . and every day after that. We soon discovered a lot in common: sense of humor, interests, perspectives, a desire to serve the church. (I did have to convert my basketball-rooting loyalties, but the relationship was worth it.) Seven months later, we were engaged, and seven months after that, we were married before God and three hundred witnesses on a cold December morning in a college chapel just outside Chicago.

On paper, it was a ministry match made in heaven. He

was studying for his Master of Divinity with an emphasis in Counseling. I was going for a Master of Arts in Christian Education with a concentration in Youth and Family Ministry. Between us, we could preach, teach, lead worship, organize, counsel, and disciple all ages. "I expect a mega-church to come out of this union," one of our seminary professors joked.

Ten years later, we stared blankly at each other across a gulf far greater than our physical distance across the kitchen. We had not produced or assisted a growing church; quite the opposite, both our current church and our marriage were slowly dying. The thing that had brought us together—a shared commitment to ministry—was now a wedge between us. How had we gotten here?

Marriage impacts calling, and calling impacts marriage, no matter what your leadership role or context is. Many of you reading this book are married. Others of you have been married at one time but are not currently. Some of you may *wish* you were married, again or for the first time. In other words, marriage (or the prospect of it) affects the majority of us sometime in our lives. So as you consider your calling, it's crucial to think through how these two life-changing commitments relate to each other. What does it look like to live out your calling in the context of marriage?

WHAT SCRIPTURE TELLS US ABOUT MARRIAGE

The Bible doesn't give many examples of how women worked out their calling, much less how they did so in the context of marriage. The dominant culture of the time was patriarchal, with men holding most positions of power within religious, political, and financial institutions. We know that men, including many kings listed in the Bible, were allowed multiple wives and concubines, while women were expected to remain faithful to one husband.[1]

When the Bible does mention specific women, they are usually either referred to without a note about their marital status or named as spouses of a central male character.[2] We know, for example, that Deborah served as a judge, although we do not know whether she was married (Judges 4); Zipporah was the wife of Moses (Exodus 2:21); Esther, a Jewish woman, was married to Xerxes, king of the Persian Empire (Esther 1); and the prophet Isaiah had a wife (Isaiah 8:3).

The New Testament provides a few more references to married women who were engaged in some type of ministry or obedience to God's call. Chief among them was Mary, who, while she was betrothed to Joseph, received word via angelic messenger that she was to be the mother of the Messiah. We know from the Bible that Mary and Joseph did marry, and that Mary was a consistent presence throughout Jesus' life, but we do not know details about her marriage or ministry.

In the Gospels, we also see that Peter was married, as Matthew tells us that Jesus healed his mother-in-law (Matthew 8:14-15). Paul later notes that Peter's wife accompanied him on some of their missionary journeys (1 Corinthians 9:5), although again, we do not know her role in Peter's ministry, or whether she had her own ministry on these trips.

In the book of Acts, we see two notable examples of married

couples involved in the early church. The more notorious of these are Ananias and his wife, Sapphira, who conspired to lie to Peter about the amount of money they received for a piece of property they sold and subsequently donated to the church (Acts 5:1-10). Joined together in untruth, they also joined each other in death for their dishonesty.

The more positive example is Priscilla and Aquila, who were expelled from Rome and settled in Corinth. There, they became hosts and trusted coworkers of Paul (Acts 18:3, 18; Romans 16:3), eventually traveling with him to Ephesus, where they together explained the "way of God" to the gifted speaker Apollos (Acts 18:24-26). Priscilla and Aquila were clearly a couple unified in their passion for and ministry in the gospel. They are always mentioned in tandem, and neither is given precedence over the other in the biblical record. Of the six references to this couple in Scripture, Priscilla is mentioned first in three of them, and Aquila first in the other three.[3]

Although the Bible is neither especially descriptive or prescriptive regarding the specific calling or ministry of married women, there are several places in the Bible where we can find teaching and principles about marriage in general that can be applied to women in ministry.

The Created Standard and Jesus' Teaching

The first biblical mention of marital union can be found in Genesis 2. Following a description of the creation of woman so that man will not be alone, the Bible states, "That is why a man leaves his father and mother and is united to his wife, and they become one flesh" (Genesis 2:24).

This understanding of marriage was reinforced by Jesus, who quoted this verse to Pharisees who quizzed him about divorce (Matthew 19:3-5). About the marriage relationship, Jesus commanded, "Therefore what God has joined together, let no one separate" (Matthew 19:6), adding that while Moses permitted divorce, it was not the created ideal.

In other words, the institution of marriage was established by God. As such, it is intended to be permanent, sacred, intimate, mutual, and exclusive.[4] Any question of calling—for *either* spouse—must be subordinate to the foundational biblical teaching about marriage.

Paul's Teaching

Paul was single, and he viewed his unmarried status as a gift (1 Corinthians 7:7). Indeed, considering his travels and travails as a missionary, we can imagine how challenging it would have been for him to be married—or for a woman to be married to him. Still, Paul respected the institution of marriage, offering his own perspective on the marriage relationship in his first letter to the church at Corinth.

Among his instructions, Paul notes that believers are free to not marry, but that those who do marry should fulfill their marital duties. Namely, husbands and wives must submit to one another and should not withhold sexual intimacy except by mutual decision in favor of a season of prayer. Paul also provides direction for husbands and wives whose spouses are not believers or have left the relationship.

It is important to note that Paul points out several times that he is not speaking for the Lord but giving his own counsel regarding marriage (1 Corinthians 7:8, 10, 12). However,

Paul's teaching does not contradict Jesus' teaching; rather, he provides additional guidance for specific situations.

Instructions Regarding Relationships

When looking at what the Bible says about marriage, we shouldn't neglect the commands regarding a Christian's behavior in relationship to others, which certainly must be practiced within a marriage relationship. For example:

- Demonstrate the fruits of the Spirit (Galatians 5:22-23).
- Do not let the sun go down while you are still angry (Ephesians 4:26).
- Keep your tongue in check (James 3:1-12).
- Do everything in love (1 Corinthians 16:14).

In addition, the "one anothers" of the Bible also apply to the marriage relationship. For example, spouses who profess faith in Christ should "bear one another's burdens" (Galatians 6:2, NASB), "forgive one another" (Colossians 3:13), "serve one another" (Galatians 5:13), "encourage one another" (1 Thessalonians 5:11), "speak truth" to one another (Ephesians 4:25), and "pray for one another" (James 5:16, NASB).

IS MARRIAGE A CALLING?

So, is marriage a calling? Yes and no.

As we see in Scripture, marriage is a covenant commitment entered into before God. By making that commitment, you take on the responsibility of tending to your marriage and loving and honoring your spouse. In that way, marriage becomes a part of your calling to fulfill your duties. Although the responsibilities of marriage must take priority over other ministry, marriage is not a more important or "spiritual" calling than singleness.

Marriage also plays a role in a woman's "corporate calling" toward Christlikeness. The intimate nature of a marriage relationship exposes our rough edges and our sinful tendencies, providing constant opportunities to grow and to give and receive grace. Indeed, as Gary Thomas writes in *Sacred Marriage*, "Any situation that calls me to confront my selfishness has enormous spiritual value, and I slowly began to understand that the real purpose of marriage may not be happiness as much as it is holiness."[5] That growth toward Christlikeness impacts our calling both in the process of discerning it and in the practice of living it out.

The commitment to marriage does not automatically replace or negate a secondary or specific calling. The Bible never says that a married woman cannot be called to other ministry; in fact, Scripture gives us Deborah and Priscilla as examples of women who had a ministry calling outside of marriage. In addition, the author of Proverbs notes that a wife of noble character cares for her family and serves those outside her home (Proverbs 31:30-31).

Some women may feel that marriage *is* their specific calling. Many other women experience a calling separate from their marriage. On the other hand, a secondary calling should remain just that in relation to one's marriage. Marriage is a covenant commitment; ministry, no matter what kind, is not. Represented visually, here is the order of priority for calling and marriage:

Christ's primary/general calling to follow him.

....

The covenant commitment of marriage.

....

A possible secondary/specific calling.

....

Your marriage should never cause you to compromise your commitment to follow Christ. But by the same token, your specific calling should never cause you to compromise your commitment to your spouse. If you are married, your marriage *is* your main ministry. Not only do you minister to your spouse through the daily interaction of marriage but you also minister to your church and community by modeling a God-honoring marriage.

In short, before considering how a particular secondary calling might play out in your marriage, it is essential to develop not just an understanding but a deep *conviction* about the proper priority of marriage as it relates to your relationship to Christ and to any possible secondary or specific calling you may experience or explore.

"I doubt that God would call you into anything that would work against your primary calling to be a mom and a wife," affirms ministry leader and author Sherry Surratt. "Sometimes, women don't want to hear that. God will never call you into something that will wreck your family because there's no way that we will stand before God and he will say, 'Too bad about your marriage, but way to go in ministry.' If you are married, that is your first calling."

Sometimes, a woman may determine that the opportunity

for marriage supersedes any previous secondary calling to ministry. Sydney was a college student who for years had planned on full-time missionary service, potentially in Nicaragua. But a reconnection with a friend from high school quickly led to romance and a marriage proposal. The thing was, the young man was committed to military service—nowhere near Nicaragua.

"When my husband proposed, I became so confused," Sydney recalled. "I tried really hard to discern between the desires of my heart and what I was really called to do. I felt like the more spiritual option was to go to the mission field. How would God tell me that it's okay to get married instead of serving him overseas?"

After much prayer, Sydney and her fiancé met with a couple at her mission agency, who reassured them that marriage was a legitimate, God-honoring option. "Afterward, I felt like a huge weight had been removed," Sydney said. "I knew that my calling to missions had not changed; it had just been paused.

"On our wedding day, I had 100 percent peace," she continued. "There was not a single doubt or question in my mind that this was where we were supposed to be. But what's crazy is that I felt the same way about Nicaragua." Sydney's heart for missions has not gone away. "I still definitely feel that pull to missions, I just don't know when or how yet. It hasn't left me, but my mission right now is my husband," she said. The commitment to marriage supersedes a secondary call to ministry, although God may also revive your secondary calling at some point down the road in the context of your marriage.

SITUATIONS AND SOLUTIONS

Dave and I had married six months before we graduated from seminary, and we quickly began to ponder and pray about where God might lead us after graduation. I initially fielded more interviews and job offers. I think this was because I was applying for youth-ministry jobs, which were more plentiful. Dave was supportive as I talked with churches around the country. But I had a growing internal sense—I believe from the Holy Spirit—that we should move for Dave's employment, not mine. While I felt called to youth ministry in general, he felt called to pastoral ministry in a local church. As we continued to pray together, God opened an opportunity for Dave to serve as an associate pastor at a church just outside St. Paul, Minnesota. We figured I would soon be able to also find work in such a large city.

I should note that my model for marriage and ministry was my youth pastor and his wife, dear friends who have now served together (still in effective youth ministry!) for over forty years. I dreamed of colaboring with my husband at a local church, sharing all the daily joys and challenges of full-time occupational ministry.

The reality was much different because, of course, Dave and I, our callings, our gifts, our personalities, and our marriage were all very different from my youth pastor and his wife. Dave and I also came into our marriage with different expectations of what the combination of ministry and marriage would look like. We didn't discuss our expectations at the time because we didn't realize them until later. This combination of differences, coupled with our individual, unrealized relational unhealth, caused very small cracks to begin forming in our marriage.

Of course, the ideal for marriage is that both spouses are in love with Jesus and with each other, and that they are always in agreement about the path forward. (Cue the sunny skies and the singing birds.) But the reality is that we are human beings, prone to sin and selfishness. These tendencies don't go away when we cross the threshold of marriage. Quite the opposite. They become even more apparent, affecting every aspect of life together—including the working out of our calling in the context of marriage.

How should we approach practical, personal issues of calling and marriage? Because the Bible does not give much specific direction on this subject, there is a good bit of space for "inferred theology" in these situations. Specific solutions will sometimes depend on your understanding of the Bible's teaching about gender roles in marriage and ministry. Because our relationship with our spouse so directly impacts any other secondary calling we may have, it's also important for us to wrestle with the implications for our unique situation. In order to help us with this critical task, I want to present a variety of real-life situations, along with suggestions of biblical principles that might apply, followed by examples of many other wise, godly women who have faced similar issues.

What If My Spouse Is Not Supportive of My Calling?

If this is your situation, let me extend to you my compassion. It is deeply discouraging to feel that God has placed within you a particular calling or passion—something you "can't not do"—not shared or supported by your life partner.

The way forward depends on the reasons behind your spouse's lack of support, which means that ascertaining these reasons is a key step in knowing how to proceed. Listen and learn, seeking to truly understand his perspective, not just to convince him of yours. At the same time, spend significant time in prayer, asking God for clarity about your perceived calling and your next steps. Enlist trusted friends to pray with you, as well. It is not outside the realm of possibility that your passion could be overshadowing your perspective and wisdom. Pursue and consider wise counsel, including from your spouse.

If your spouse is not a follower of Christ, remember that how you handle this situation will be a primary means of witness to him. Although your specific calling feels very strong, remember the priority of your covenant commitment to your spouse. Run toward the relationship and always seek to be an example of Christlike love. If your spouse is a Christian, pray together for clarity and unity, trusting that God will make the path clear in his right timing.

If your spouse is not wholeheartedly supportive, you may consider asking for permission to explore your calling, perhaps for a temporary time period or an intermediate step. If this arrangement is agreeable to both of you, remain in prayer with the Lord and in close conversation with each other during the process.

Kate is a forty-four-year-old mother of three older teenagers. As she considers the impending empty biological nest, she feels a strong calling toward foster care. Kate's husband, a strong Christian, does not share this sense of calling, however. Kate described her state as an internal tension of "knowing the future, but not the path."

"What I feel that God is asking me to do is not something I can decide to do in isolation," Kate said. "It would be a decision for my whole family. I cannot expect my husband to jump in with both feet, eager to serve in a way that causes our finances and lifestyle to shift, without him being willing or feeling called to do so.

"Our marriage is a partnership, and we cannot make decisions apart from one another. We are one," Kate continued. "So, I am in the most painful stage of calling: waiting. I cannot move forward without my husband, and I cannot go back to where I was before (in my prayers and thinking) and be at peace. I must prayerfully wait to see what the Lord will do next. He is *always* at his work."

The bottom line is that obedience to God's calling begins with faithfulness to your marriage vows. God wants to shape you through the discipleship process more than he needs to use you for a particular task elsewhere in the world.

What If I Am Called to Occupational Ministry[6] and My Spouse Is Not?

Although this situation sounds similar to the first one, it differs in one significant regard: In this case, a spouse is supportive overall but does not share the same occupational calling. The potential tension here lies not in dealing with misalignment in support but in working out possibilities and practicalities as a married couple.

Potential solutions in this situation will stem in part from a couple's shared understanding of gender roles in marriage and ministry. Depending on perspective, a couple may decide to close doors to particular roles (for example, serving as a pastor in a church) or types of organizations. Once those parameters have been determined, couples still have many options from which to choose.

Many couples have chosen the option of a "trailing spouse," where they decide to pursue one person's vocation, trusting that God will also provide opportunities for the other partner. Jenni and her husband have been married nineteen years. For the majority of their marriage, they have moved for Jenni's jobs in local-church ministry. Ashley and her husband also decided to move for her job after she graduated from seminary.

On the flip side, Marlena has chosen to be the trailing spouse to her husband, whose opportunities as a philosophy professor are far more limited. Marlena currently serves as director of discipleship at a local church near her husband's university. "We go according to his job, and I just try to figure it out from there," she said. "We feel called together, and he said he would be willing to move for me in an instant, but the problem is that if he were to leave his tenure-track position for me, he may not be able to find work elsewhere." At the same time, she admits that at times it is hard being "tethered" to his job.

A larger city usually provides more possibilities for both spouses to find meaningful work. Although both Jenni's and Ashley's husbands chose the "trailing" role in terms of initial job placement, neither had any problem finding work in their occupations in their respective cities of Nashville and Los Angeles. The "trailing" issue becomes more challenging in a smaller town.

As with any issue or decision in marriage, the key is open, honest, and regular communication about not just specific options but also the shared values and principles that will help guide a couple through situations and decisions.

What If Both of Us Are Called to Occupational Ministry?

Spouses who both feel called to occupational ministry must navigate their own unique challenges. Marriage sometimes creates more opportunities for spouses; other times, it can place more restrictions on how, when, and where they work out their calling.

Again, some couples choose the "trailing spouse" approach, with one spouse's calling given priority in decisions of geographic location, time allotment, and parenting roles. Options may once again depend on convictions about gender roles. Solutions may also vary depending on seasons of life, a topic we will examine more closely in the next chapter.

Thirty-year-old Caroline and her husband recently worked through these questions as they contemplated their first move as a married couple after meeting in seminary, where they both prepared for pastoral ministry. "This is the first time we've ever had to think of a call jointly," she said. "A few months ago, I interviewed at a church in a small town in the southeast for an associate pastor position. I really liked the senior pastor, I really liked the committee, and I was very interested in learning more. But [my husband] and I asked ourselves: If we moved there, what would he do?

"Through that process, I was the one who said, 'I don't want to move somewhere where you don't have the potential to find meaningful work,'" Caroline continued. "I backed out of the search process. I knew I was their top candidate, it was a lot closer to family, and I would have been doing what I want to do. As difficult as that was, I felt good about the decision." Several months later, Caroline and her husband were offered pastoral positions in different churches in the same city in North Carolina, less than thirty minutes from her family.

When both spouses feel called to occupational ministry, one important issue for them to discuss is their conviction regarding worship together as a family unit. For Dave and me, being a part of the same faith community is a non-negotiable "stake in the ground" based on our ecclesiology (beliefs about the nature and purpose of the church), our views on marriage, and our understanding of corporate calling. This conviction has definitely limited my opportunities for ministry. Other godly couples have navigated this question differently.

When both spouses are engaged in occupational ministry, several possible scenarios fall under the general categories of "ministry together" and "ministry apart." Each brings a unique set of questions and challenges.

MINISTRY TOGETHER

Ministry together means that both spouses serve within the same organization. The dynamics of ministry together involve two components: (1) organizational structure, and (2) individual personality and gifts. Many organizations have policies regarding the potential roles and relationships of family members, although these policies may vary widely.

For example, one church might not hire multiple family members. Another may hire members of the same family, but only in separate departments or situations in which one does not report to the other. Still another may actively encourage familial employment. Each approach has valid reasons as well as potential benefits and drawbacks. Regardless of an organization's chosen approach, a couple ministering together will be impacted by these policies and structures.

Each spouse's personality and gifts affect what ministry together looks like as well. Even if spousal co-employment is permitted, it may not be beneficial to a marriage. Some couples do well ministering together; others need more space from each other.

"My husband and I both have a passion for mission, for his gifts are in connecting with people one-on-one and through encouragement, while mine are teaching and leading," shared Sarah. "God is the one who set us up with these gifts, so saying my husband has to lead because he is the husband doesn't seem to fit. At the same time, I'm not the sort of person who will strongly lead and expect my husband to follow. Working together as equals on a team when others lead has worked fine, as has working as equals without a team. In the end, though, working in different ministries seems to be healthier for our marriage."

Some couples find that both their marriage and their ministry flourish when they serve and lead in close partnership. This is not the case for Dave and me. In addition to agreeing never again to work together on a household-painting project, Dave and I have realized that we do best when we have "his, mine, and ours" components to our ministry. The "his" is pastoral ministry, specifically preaching and pastoral care, in a local church. The "mine" is teaching and leadership for the larger church, while remaining rooted in our local community of faith. The "ours" is shared hospitality. We regularly host people in our home, whether families, groups of teens, or ministry teams. We also talk a lot about ministry.

MINISTRY APART

Some couples may serve in different organizations in the same geographic locale. Occupational ministry, as those of us engaged in it know all too well, does not fall within neat schedules. That means there can be a lot of flexibility but also a lot of competing time demands. Couples in this situation need to determine how they will protect and grow their marriage, taking advantage of the flexibility to meet and manage the demands.

Teresa is a licensed professional counselor and director of a counseling clinic, while her husband is the senior pastor of a large, multisite church. For them, each season of life has required a different strategy for managing their schedules and maintaining their marriage.

"We used to have to get away," explained Teresa, who is now an empty nester. "When our kids were little, oftentimes, we would go weeks without any real time together except for what I call functional conversations, which can put your marriage on fumes really fast. So for one weekend a month, we would go to a cabin thirty minutes away and literally unplug. We always had to have two nights away. The first night we either slept or fought, and the second night was our real connection time."

In addition to their weekend getaways when their children were younger, Teresa and her husband took advantage of any possible connection time: dinner once a week, an hour together here or there, driving instead of flying in order to enjoy extended conversation time in the car. These days, the couple walks together almost every morning. "That has been huge relational time, such a gift," she noted.

Teresa is involved in the church her husband pastors, but she has found her own niche, serving as a teacher and volunteer in various ministries. She has also found community outside the church. "I've always been a part of a Bible study where I'm not the pastor's wife, because everywhere at church, I'm 'Rick's wife,'" Teresa explained. "It's so important for me to have a place where I can just be 'Teresa.'

"I don't know that we've done anything special," she continued. "All I can say is that it's been a journey, we've had to work at it, and it hasn't always been pretty. It has involved a lot of creativity, and a lot of help from other people along the way."

Other couples find themselves separated, for various reasons, by geographic distance. While this arrangement allows more time to focus on work, it requires concentrated effort by both partners to maintain emotional connection across the miles. Sometimes a "for now" arrangement requiring physical distance is necessary. Without tremendous intentionality, however, "for now" could become "for too long" or "forever."

Susan and her husband have been married for thirty-five years and geographically separated for the last two. They decided together that he would move to begin a new role at a seminary near his aging mother in Colorado, while she would remain in Illinois to complete several major projects at her church and to be near several of their children and grandchildren. In addition to regular phone and video calls, Susan and her husband see each other once or twice a month. Susan's words are a reminder of the difficulty of their decision.

"I would never recommend what we're doing. It's not ideal. It's just for a season, and it's a unique season. If we were younger, or if we had different personalities, it would be much more stressful," she said. "We prayed about this two years ago and asked, do we just shut the door on his opportunity, or do we pick up and leave? But I did not have a sense of closure for my work here."

Susan continued, "Do we miss being with each other? Definitely. It's hard. I like to think that I try to keep my hands open, but at this point, I don't feel released from here." At the same time, Susan noted that their personalities have helped make the arrangement work. "We are better together, but we are also healthy apart," she said. "Not everyone can understand that, because it doesn't look like the traditional marriage model. One shoe doesn't fit all people. You really have to be in tune with your marriage because [this situation] does not work for everybody."

DECIDING TOGETHER

We moved to Minnesota and Dave happily went off to work, fulfilled in his pastoral position. Meanwhile, I struggled to fulfill my own calling. We didn't realize it at the time, but Dave's role as pastor led to fewer opportunities for me, not more.

When Dave got his offer of employment from the church, we were a bit surprised to see that the terms of his employment included that I not work at another church. We understood and agreed with the rationale that we should worship and serve together, so we readily accepted these terms. But this limited my occupational-ministry opportunities to either our own church or a youth-related nonprofit.

A few years later, I was asked to work with the high-school ministry at our church. I was absolutely thrilled, and I have been told that my ministry had a lasting impact on the lives of students, parents, and leaders. The catch was that because of church policy and Dave's pastoral position, I had to be referred to (and paid as) an intern, even though I had a master's degree in youth ministry. I was assured that the policy would be reviewed, however, and that I would soon be recognized as a fully contributing staff member.

Instead, several months later, I was told that the committee had decided against the policy change. The reason I was given was that the committee was concerned that if both Dave and I were on staff and one of us left for another organization, both of us would leave. I was hurt and frustrated—I felt that I had been told I couldn't do ministry at my church, but I couldn't do it elsewhere, either.

(Ironically, that decision and Dave's support of me was one catalyst for us to leave that church, so the committee's fear ended up being realized, although not in the way they anticipated.)

From Minnesota, we moved to a much smaller church in a metropolitan area in North Carolina, where Dave served as the solo pastor. Again, I had a hard time figuring out where

I could fulfill my calling as a ministry leader. Because of this church's size, there was not a good place for me to lead in the church without it looking like a mom-and-pop operation. Dave and I also have very different leadership styles; working very closely together, as I had originally envisioned, just led to significant frustration for both of us.

Meanwhile, our small and struggling church was becoming smaller and struggling-er. I wanted to apply my leadership gifts to help but felt constrained. Dave was facing his worst fear: "failure" as a pastor of a declining church. What had been the first connection between us—a shared calling to ministry—now divided us. We felt we could no longer talk with the other about the thing—the *life*—that was so important to both of us. I developed anxiety that escalated for months, until I finally crashed into clinical depression.

It was at this point that we faced each other across the kitchen, wondering how we had grown so far apart. Dave felt that I had abandoned him in his struggle to save the church, and I felt that he had abandoned me as he focused on the church instead of caring for me during my illness. There are few things worse than sleeping in the same bed with your spouse and yet feeling utterly alone.

One day, in desperation, Dave went for a walk in the woods to talk to God about our situation. He was looking for a solution to the issues at the church. The message he got instead was that our marriage needed to win at all costs. He came home and told me that he realized he needed to step down from his position at the church, even though we didn't have a solid job offer or clear next step. For the first time in years, I felt a glimmer of hope. By that point, I didn't care about our ministry dreams; I just wanted Dave and me to be *unified* again.

Every couple will face significant decisions if one or both spouses sense some type of calling. Approaching these decisions with forethought and intentionality is vital for a marriage to remain healthy in the midst of discernment and decision. Although you can't anticipate every possible scenario, it is helpful to discuss *how* you and your spouse will approach these decisions. It is often easier to lay down shared commitments before having to apply them to real-life, high-stakes decisions. What are some principles and practices to guide couples in this situation?

Trust the Holy Spirit

Jana and her husband are folk musicians who minister around the world with their young-adult children. Their path started with their understanding of marriage and calling. "We realized that our marriage was actually God weaving us together in the body of Christ first and foremost," Jana explained. "How would we honor that and participate in the body of Christ together, in covenant?"

To discern their next steps, Jana and her family trust the stirrings they believe God has placed in their hearts. "God sometimes gives us maps, but they are temporary," she said. "We do pray a lot, but our prayers tend to be for others. Once every year, we do a Dream Talk as a family. That's been really instrumental for us. We can see the elements that we each have on our hearts, and then we just put those before the Lord, saying, 'Hey, we all have these stirrings, so we're going to start moving toward them. If you don't want them to work out, shut the door.'

"Nine times out of ten, they work out," Jana told me. "For the most part, we tell him what we want and start moving toward it, but based on a reference point of availability and vulnerability."

Our loving Father desires what is best for us. If we have tuned our hearts to his, our desires and his will be unified. And the Holy Spirit will never fail to guide us toward God's purposes if we humbly seek his direction for our lives.

Act in Unity

Laura and her husband are in the process of beginning a retreat center for ministry leaders. "We were at lunch one day and said, 'Hey, if we had a place, what could we do with it?' By the time lunch was over, we were selling our house and building a retreat ministry, and a lot of it was my husband's input," Laura said.

For Laura and her husband, the most important guiding principle is unity. "Neither of us can make a move until we are both in it," she said. Laura has also seen God use her and her husband's personalities in the discernment process. "My husband is usually reserved, and I'm the one with the crazy ideas," she explained. "It's pretty affirming when he is the one with the crazy ideas. Then I know this might be from God."

In our marriage, I am also usually the first to sense a nudge regarding a direction or decision. Sometimes, I want to force Dave to come on board with whatever I am sensing. But I have learned to trust that if the direction is of God, he will also direct Dave. Trust in God's gifts to you through your spouse, and wait for unity in God's direction.

Make Space to Listen

Laura and her husband understand how vital it is to take space to hear God. "If we don't slow down long enough to really listen, then we don't ever hear what God is trying to say," she said. "Even with this retreat ministry, we were having some trouble discerning our next steps. It took the two of us taking time away to just talk about it and listen to what God was speaking to each of us individually. We move at such a fast pace sometimes. If we don't slow down, we can't really hear."

Intentional time and space away to listen to God is a critical component to mutual discernment. One way to do this is to take a silent retreat, a practice my husband and I learned from our friends Dave and Ellen. Ellen explained:

> When Dave and I have a big decision to make—
> something that will alter both of our lives—we bank
> on James 1:5, which says, "If you need wisdom,
> ask our generous God, and he will give it to you."[7]
> We've done these retreats about big decisions when
> we knew we needed God's intervention, because
> without it, there was no way we could know what
> the right answer was, or maybe there wasn't a "right"
> answer. The decision is not necessarily something we
> disagree on, it's just a big decision we need to make,
> and we want to make sure we are headed in the right
> direction when we make it.

In preparation for their personal retreat time, Dave and Ellen enlist the prayers of trusted friends before and during the retreat day. On the day of the retreat, the questions she and her husband ask God depend on the situation.

In the same way, every time Dave and I have faced significant decisions related to our direction or future, we each go to a separate place for a predetermined time to pray, reflect on Scripture, and journal. Dave often goes for a walk, while I usually hole up in a quiet corner of a library or bookstore.

Sometimes we have an agreed-upon question or issue for which we are seeking the Lord's guidance. Other times, each of us has our own questions, and still other times, we head out without any specific questions and just ask God to speak to us. After we have spent individual time with the Lord, we get together to talk about what we have heard. It never fails to amaze me that each time we have done this exercise, we have come back together having received the same answer or direction from God, even when we haven't asked the same questions.

Making space to hear from God as a couple benefits your relationship with God and with your spouse. As Ellen put it, "I've learned that when I go into these times with God, I need to be open to hearing *anything*. God wants to give direction, but he might want to give sustaining words of hope. I have had times where I haven't heard anything big; I just spent a lot of time in prayer and Bible study and journaling. That's still time spent with God, and that time benefited me even though I didn't hear a big 'aha.' It's never a time that is worthless."

HEALTHY MARRIAGE, HEALTHY CALLING

For Dave and me, that day in the kitchen marked the start of a long, difficult journey of examination and repair in our marriage. Both of us needed to repent of a variety of sins that had hurt our marriage, even while our external ministry had been fruitful. We finally had the scary, honest talks that we had skirted for too long. We stepped on each other's toes as we tried to learn new relational dance patterns. There were times when loving each other was a minute-by-minute choice. We wondered if it would ever get easier.

It did. Eventually, and ever so slowly, but it did. It was one of those seasons that we would never want to go through again but that we wouldn't trade for anything. We emerged stronger, better, and healthier as individuals, as a couple, and in our relationship with Christ. We recently celebrated our twenty-fourth wedding anniversary with a warm-weather getaway. (Indiana gets cold in December, y'all.) We are thriving individually and as a couple, in our marriage and in ministry. We are grateful that our long, hard season is now but a distant speck in the rearview mirror. Along the way, we have both learned a lot about ourselves and about what it looks like to fulfill our callings in the context of marriage.

As Dave and I can both testify, the health of your marriage directly influences the health of your ministry. A strong marriage provides the foundation for both spouses to more effectively fulfill their respective callings. And no matter how long you have been married, there are no shortcuts to a healthy, strong relationship.

WHAT NOW?

As you consider how to approach this intersection between calling and marriage, here are a few things to keep in mind.

First, *marriage is a big deal.* It is an institution created by God. Apart from a woman's relationship to Christ, marriage is the most important commitment she can make. It affects internal spiritual formation and external ministry. This is why marriage should be entered into "reverently, discreetly, advisedly, soberly, and in the fear of God."[8]

Second, *remember that every marriage is different.* While every marriage is a covenant commitment before God, each marriage is unique in how spouses walk the path of relationship with each other, with God, and with the question of calling. It was very freeing for my husband and me to be told by a marriage counselor that there are a lot of "right" ways to work things out in a marriage.

The application of this truth? Don't compare. You and your spouse need to navigate your own course for your marriage under God's authority. It is helpful to learn from the examples of other couples, but don't accept pressure to make your marriage look like any other.

Third, *keep the correct priority.* Your marriage should be subject to your primary calling to follow Christ, and your secondary calling should never come before your marriage. Fulfill your covenant commitment to your spouse by making your marriage a priority. Can you say that your marriage is your greatest achievement?

Drive this stake into the ground: No external ministry is worth a failed (or ailing) marriage. **Do whatever you need to** do to make your marriage your strongest ministry. Repeat and renew your marriage vows every day. Invite mature Christian couples to speak into your lives. Seek professional marriage counseling when needed (or even better, before).

A CODA: CALLING AS A SINGLE WOMAN

Now to the unmarried and the widows I say:
It is good for them to stay unmarried.
THE APOSTLE PAUL, I CORINTHIANS 7:8

If you are reading this chapter as someone who is not married, I want to take some time to speak directly to you. According to 2012 census data, only about half of the U.S. adult population is married.[9] Unfortunately, single adults are still viewed as second-class citizens in many Christian communities, even though Paul refers to singleness as a unique gift.

Our cultural terminology reflects this perceived hierarchy. Those of us who are married talk about our "better half" or say that marriage "completes us," implying (usually unintentionally) that single people are not whole on their own. We also often confer greater leadership credibility to a married person, even though life experience alone does not guarantee maturity.

But as more adults are marrying later (or not at all), the Christian community needs to reevaluate its perspective of singleness, recognizing the significant contributions that singles of all ages can make to the church—and not just as volunteers during marriage-enrichment events. At the same time, single women should not put unbalanced weight on marriage, expecting it to make them feel complete or useful.

A woman who is not content in singleness will not suddenly become content in marriage, and all women are called to faithfulness, regardless of their marital status. Katelyn Beaty writes, "As it turns out, I was and am responsible for making the most of the time God has given me in this life, with or without a spouse."[10]

Andrea is a twenty-eight-year-old single woman who teaches math at a Christian school in Nicaragua. Although she is open to marriage, right now she is very content, even thankful, to be single.

"Overall, I tend to cherish my singleness and recognize what a blessing it can be," she said. "I don't want this to sound cavalier or like I hate marriage, but I am so happy that I'm single because in some ways, I feel like it makes things easier for me.

"When I felt a calling here, I didn't have to pray with my partner and say, 'Do you feel this, too?'" Andrea explained. "It's just between me and God. And knowing me and my personality, it's probably good it's just between me and God because if I were married and had a husband here, I'd probably be leaning on him more than on God. I'm a people person and like to talk to people out loud, so I would be pouring out my heart to him, not to God.

"A lot of people here say, 'We've got to find you a man.' I ask them, 'What makes you think I need someone?' If God brings someone, it will be obvious," she said. "But if this is my calling, that's great. I choose to focus on the blessings of it and steer clear of the negative mind-set because God has proven to me that he can work in and through me even as a single person."

We should never think of singleness as "less than." Yes, this chapter has been about marriage. Yes, marriage is a big deal. But no, marriage is not for everybody. It is challenging and, in some ways, limiting. Focus on obedience to Christ, wherever he leads and whatever your marital status.

CONTINUE THE CONVERSATION

» On a scale of 1–10, with 10 being high and 1 being low, how well do you feel you and your spouse are currently communicating about issues related to calling?

» What assumptions or expectations did you bring into your marriage relating to your own or your spouse's calling?

» In what order have you prioritized your callings (general, marriage, specific)? Do you feel that the order in your life needs some adjustment?

» Which situations and stories in this chapter resonated with you? What big questions are you facing, personally and as a couple?

» What principles and practices can you apply that might bring some resolution to these questions?

Chapter 5

CALLING AND SEASONS OF LIFE

I had work to do, and my infant son was not cooperating.

During the first year of my first son's life, I worked two part-time jobs: one as director of the high-school ministry at our church, and the other as a mentor to seminary students preparing for youth ministry. This was one of my work-at-home days, when I would set up my laptop at the dining-room table and squeeze in a few hours of planning and emails while my son took his afternoon nap. It was a great arrangement.

Except that my son was not sleeping.

As I listened to him babble through the baby monitor, I felt my stress level rising. He was supposed to sleep for at least another hour. I had a lot to do. I cherished this quiet interlude, and now this inconsiderate, needy, noisy little creature was cutting it short.

Don't you know I have work to do? I thought angrily. My heart exploded in resentment toward my son. A moment later, I was flooded with shame.

Was I truly mad at a *six-month-old* for not following *my* schedule?

It was certainly not my proudest moment.

(In our family, we joke that our kids' therapy funds are bigger than their college funds. I'm sure you can see why.)

As embarrassing as that story now feels, the tension I felt in that season of life was very, very real. Part of me wanted to be a stay-at-home mom with my young children. But an equal part of me wanted—no, needed—work and ministry outside the home. I still felt called to ministry, and now I also felt called to the responsibility of motherhood. And I had no idea how (or even whether) the two were supposed to work together. I felt so *divided*, and I hated that feeling.

Whatever your age and life stage, the reality is that seasons of life affect a woman's call to ministry. What are these seasons, how do they affect our calling, and what principles should guide us as we seek to navigate these challenges as leaders?

A TIME FOR EVERYTHING

The Bible mentions infants; children; youth; men and women who are young, "older," and old; parents; and grandparents. As with calling and marriage, Scripture does not give much specific instruction about the relationship between calling and age or life stage.

The Bible *is* clear from example, however, that God can

CALLING AND SEASONS OF LIFE

use people of all ages, even children, for his Kingdom purposes. Samuel was just a toddler when he began instruction under Eli, the high priest; at around age eleven or twelve, Samuel heard God call him personally (1 Samuel 1:21-28; 3).[1] Several decades later, Samuel anointed David, youngest son of Jesse, as the successor to Saul as king of Israel (1 Samuel 16:1-13). Jehoash (Joash) was only seven years old when he became king of Judah (2 Kings 11:21), and Josiah was eight when he took the throne several generations later (2 Kings 22:1).

God also profoundly used people who were considered past the typical age of productivity; in other words, they were *old*. Noah was six hundred when he entered the ark he had built to house his family and animals during the Flood; afterward, he lived to the ripe old age of nine hundred and fifty (Genesis 7:6; 9:29)! Sarah was ninety when God promised Abraham that she would bear a son, and Isaac was born when Abraham was one hundred (Genesis 17:17; 21:5). And Moses was eighty years old (and his brother, Aaron, eighty-three) when they first asked Pharaoh to release the Israelites from slavery in Egypt (Exodus 7:7).

Compared to these examples, Jesus was a rather pedestrian thirty years old when he began his earthly ministry (Luke 3:23). Interestingly, our Savior is one of very few characters whose exact age is noted in the New Testament record, although cultural and historical factors indicate that the original disciples were also young men when they first accepted Jesus' call to follow him.[2]

Although we do not know Paul's age at his conversion or at various points during his ministry, the apostle provides several specific instructions related to age and ministry. To Timothy, his spiritual son, Paul writes, "Don't let anyone look down on you because you are young, but set an example for the believers in speech, in conduct, in love, in faith and in purity" (1 Timothy 4:12). And in his letter to church leader Titus, Paul explains that older women should teach younger women the ways of faith and family (Titus 2:3-5).

In addition to these examples and teaching, throughout Scripture, we see the key theme of *seasons* that applies to all life, whether plants, animals, or human beings. "There is a time for everything, and a season for every activity under the heavens," writes the author of Ecclesiastes (Ecclesiastes 3:1). These seasons include:

> a time to be born and a time to die,
> a time to plant and a time to uproot,
> a time to kill and a time to heal,
> a time to tear down and a time to build,
> a time to weep and a time to laugh,
> a time to mourn and a time to dance,
> a time to scatter stones and a time to gather them,
> a time to embrace and a time to reframe from
>   embracing,
> a time to search and a time to give up,
> a time to keep and a time to throw away,
> a time to tear and a time to mend,
> a time to be silent and a time to speak,
> a time to love and a time to hate,
> a time for war and a time for peace.
>
> ECCLESIASTES 3:2-8

In addition, God instituted seasons of rest, from the Sabbath (Exodus 20:10) to Sabbaticals for cancelling debt (Deuteronomy 15:1) to Years of Jubilee (Leviticus 25:8-13). Finally, the Bible references seasons of a woman's life—girl, young woman, old woman; and singleness, marriage, and widowhood—and gives examples of women who followed God in each of these seasons. Thus, from biblical teaching, examples, and principles, we see that while age and life stage are not qualifiers (or disqualifiers) for receiving a call from God, they do affect the working out of that call.

SEASONS OF A WOMAN'S LIFE

The broad seasons of a woman leader's life include young adulthood, middle age, and the senior years. God can call anyone to anything at any age (check out Sarah's pregnancy at age ninety!), but each season impacts a woman's ability and availability to follow God's calling. Let's look at the specifics of each season, including advantages, challenges, and keys to navigating that season.

Young Adulthood

Generally, young adulthood begins in a woman's late teen years and continues through her twenties and early thirties, although some researchers extend young adulthood to age forty.[3] At the start of this season, women usually have more physical energy but fewer financial resources. If they are single or do not have children, they may also have more autonomy over their time.

Young adulthood is a season of discovery for both men

and women: of who they are, of what they want to do with their life, of how they want to spend their time, and with whom they want to spend that time. These are significant issues, and working through them can feel overwhelming.

"A rarely discussed secret is that almost all of us flail through our twenties," writes Jennie Allen. "One big reason is that we don't know ourselves yet.

"We are just barely learning

- what we are good at;
- what we are terrible at;
- how our stories could ever be helpful to others;
- how to follow the Holy Spirit;
- how to not be a selfish brat;
- how to really love;
- what our passions are."[4]

("But to be perfectly fair," she adds, "I meet people all the time who are fifty-plus and still trying to figure it out."[5])

As these initial questions are answered, young women begin to feel more established, yet more stretched and potentially stressed by the challenge of balancing their roles and responsibilities. In regard to calling, women in this season may question whether any initial sense of calling is still valid or viable in light of changing life circumstances.

Young adulthood is a season of tremendous learning about your calling and about navigating life in general. The #adulting struggle is real, and I remember it well. In a year's time in my midtwenties, I got married, graduated from seminary, started paying back student loans, bought a car, moved a thousand miles to a new city and church, rented an apartment, then bought a house, and got a dog. Adulthood got real in a hurry. I remember writing to friends that according to those tests that measure stress factors, I should have been dead by Christmas! At the same time, I was excited to finally be out in the "real world," finding my way.

KEY TASKS FOR CALLING IN YOUNG ADULTHOOD

The first key task to successfully navigate calling in this life stage is to cultivate an ear for the Holy Spirit. Learn to recognize his voice in your life. This can only be done with practice, including intentional time away from *pursuit* in order to be fully *present* to God. Listen and learn. Ask God to continue to mold your heart to his. No other ability or task is more important than this. Embed healthy habits and disciplines now, instead of waiting until you have more time, more money, more things.

The second key task is to cultivate authentic, deep relationships with people who can speak into your life and potentially go the distance on your life journey. Plug into a local church. Invest in life-giving friendships, and learn how to be a life-giving friend to others. One of these friends might be a spouse if God directs you toward marriage—but marriage does *not* replace your need for other friendships. Get connected in *community* with people of all ages and life stages, including wise women ahead of you on the journey.

The third key task is to experiment! This is a season for trying new things as part of the process of learning who you are. A lot of movement—between ministries, jobs, homes, cities—is not unusual in this season. If something doesn't work out, don't view it as a failure; learn from it and move on. And if you find something that clicks, stick with it.

WOMEN SPEAK: LOOKING BACK

Women Over Forty: What Would You Tell Your Younger Self about Leadership and/or Ministry?

- "It's okay to say no to the 'good' so that you can give your best to the 'better.' You don't have to be all things to all people."—*Jes*

- "Don't let a closed door stop you. Sometimes doors need a push to be opened, but they aren't locked. Push that door!"—*Denise*

- "Find older mentors, and ask about their journey. And be prepared for your dreams to take a long time. You *can* do it all, but over the space of a lifetime, not all at once."—*Fran*

- "You are not crazy; you're called. Don't wait for human beings to give you permission to do what God created you to do."—*Cynthia*

- "Spend lots of time developing self-awareness about your strengths and weaknesses but more importantly, about your needs. When you know what you need to sustain yourself in ministry, you can be in it for the long haul!"—*Sarah*

- "Give yourself permission to be fallible. Understand it's not the end of the world if you fail at something."—*Val*

Middle Age

Middle age generally begins in a woman's forties and continues until her early to midsixties. The average life expectancy was only sixty-one years when the United States Social Security program was enacted in 1935.[6] It amazes me that today, *middle* age continues past the age at which most people once expected to die. Sixty really is the new forty.

Developmental psychologist Erik Erikson theorized that during this life stage, adults grapple with "generativity" (that is, making a mark on the world) versus stagnation. "We give back to society through raising our children, being productive at work, and becoming involved in community activities and organizations," explains Saul McLeod. "Through generativity we develop a sense of being a part of the bigger picture."[7]

This season of life is often marked by tremendous productivity, greater financial stability, and deeper relationships. Women in this stage often feel a strong sense of accomplishment. Having made it through the lean "starting-out" years, they are now more established both personally and professionally. They may have experienced some kind of leadership success. They have greater clarity about who God has created them to be. They feel less pressure to impress others. They know who they can trust and have developed strong emotional bonds by walking through life with those people.

Middle age can also be marked by deep pain and loss. The body begins to show signs of aging, leading to a greater awareness of personal mortality. (Many of us can attest that the body's warranty runs out at about age forty.) Some women may find themselves caring for both their children and their aging parents, then grieving the loss of the former to the empty nest and the latter to debilitation or death. Most marriages in this season have taken a lot of lumps, and not all of them have survived. Some women lament never having married. Many others' dreams may have been shattered against hard reality.

The transitions of this season also affect personal calling. As emotional, spiritual, physical, and time resources and demands change, some women experience an increase in availability and opportunity. Others decide to pause or reduce external ministry while they tend to other responsibilities. Still others discern a new or different calling altogether. Many experience all of the above over the course of this long stage of life.

As I write this, I am smack-dab in the middle of middle age. At age forty, I had two preteen boys and four healthy parents, and I rarely saw a doctor. Now as I near age fifty, I have one son in college and another headed there in a few months. My dear mother- and father-in-law both passed away nearly five years ago, and my own parents are declining rapidly. I have trifocals (excuse me, they are *progressive lenses*), a daily regimen of supplements, and a record of more "oscopies" than I care to count.

My calling journey over the last ten years reflects these life changes. A decade ago, I was finally enjoying an increase in professional opportunities as I completed my doctoral studies and my sons grew more independent in their early teens. A part-time teaching gig at a Christian graduate school eventually morphed into a full-time position that required regular travel.

Then we hit the high-school years, with their flurry of practices and meets and performances and driver's ed and fundraisers and volunteering and youth group and senior pictures and jobs and late-night talks and standardized tests and college visits and proms and a steady stream of teens through our front door. In the thick of all that, my dad was hospitalized and we lost my husband's parents, seven hundred miles away, after short but difficult illnesses.

As I sat at an out-of-state staff retreat, my phone continuously buzzing with text messages and voice mails, I realized something had to give. This time, there was no resentment. I needed and wanted to be fully present to my kids, to my husband, and to our extended family during that critical season. While my calling to occupational ministry had not changed, I felt clearly that God wanted me to press "pause" for the foreseeable future. I didn't know what would come afterward, but I knew what I needed to do in that moment. I scaled back to a part-time position, then resigned a few months later.

When the dust from that whirlwind settled a few years later, I found myself alone in a quiet house, asking God, "Now what?" I confess to fearing that I had missed some sort of window for external-ministry opportunities or my years of peak professional productivity. Within weeks, God provided an invitation to teach. Then another. Then a writing assignment. And another. As I fulfilled those assignments, God confirmed my calling to leadership development and fine-tuned it toward writing and teaching.

I now believe that some of my most significant ministry is yet to come. I look around my office and see photos of the rich cadre of friends who have walked with me for years, sometimes decades. I have more time, greater financial freedom, decent energy, a strong marriage, and a supportive spouse. My tea mug confirms: Life is Good.

In other words, middle age can be pretty awesome, but we must pursue several key tasks to successfully navigate this season.

KEY TASKS FOR CALLING IN MIDDLE AGE

The first key task on the calling journey during this life stage is to do your necessary emotional work. As you experience successes, challenges, and disappointments, allow yourself to acknowledge them and to explore your emotions in response to each. Identify your emotional triggers, your toxic interpersonal habits, your sources of greatest joy. Work through your past and present wounds so that you can pursue your calling out of healing and wholeness. I highly recommend enlisting the help of a professional therapist; seeking this type of counseling is a sign of intentionality and strength, not of weakness.

The second and related key task is to continue moving toward complete surrender to Christ. During midlife, you will experience what Janet Hagberg and Robert Guelich call "the Wall," or "our will meeting God's will face to face."[8] In other words, you will come to the hard realization (often repeatedly) that you can't control things, despite your best efforts. At this point, you are faced with a critical choice: either revert to a spirituality lived through the head and hands (learning *about* God or doing things *for* God), or push ahead and live into a new spirituality, one based in unconditional love for God, for others, and for ourselves.

Going through the Wall requires discomfort, sacrifice,

surrender, awareness, forgiveness, and acceptance—in other words, completely relinquishing any illusion of control in our lives and relationships. This spiritual transformation cannot occur without simultaneous psychological transformation. "We move toward wholeness *and* holiness," Hagberg and Guelich write.[9] Peter Scazzero, author of *Emotionally Healthy Spiritually*, declares, "It's impossible to be spiritually mature while remaining emotionally immature."[10]

Because this stage is so unsettling and difficult—indeed, it requires completely breaking our previous paradigms—many Christians choose to return to more familiar and comfortable ground, living in old patterns of relating to God, others, and themselves. *But unless you work through the Wall, your leadership will become critically stunted.* Leadership influence flows from who you are, not what you do. If you are not willing to go through the hard process of transformation in your own life, you will not be able to lead others to full emotional and spiritual health.[11]

The third key task as you progress through this season of life is to give back. Look for and invest in those behind you on the journey. Somewhere, there is someone who wants to follow you. This can happen in formal or informal mentoring relationships, either personally or long-distance. You don't have to have it all figured out; you just need to be honest about what God is teaching you. I am grateful for the women who have invested in me as I followed their footsteps and for the opportunity to now "send the elevator back down"[12] to other young men and women who are just beginning their ministry journey.

Wherever you might be in this season of life, be assured

that you potentially have *many* years of ministry impact ahead of you. "*Please* tell these forty- and fifty-year-old women that things are just getting started!" begged Cassia, who, at age forty-three, feels as though a whole new world has opened up; she is working toward a seminary degree and planting seeds for a God-directed writing and teaching ministry, even while preparing two teens to leave the nest. Indeed, many women report that despite initial fears of life ending at age forty, middle age ends up being their favorite season of life.

The Senior Years

This season generally begins in a woman's midsixties and continues until she departs this world. Given continued

LEADERSHIP FOR THE LONG HAUL

To reflect on your potential leadership legacy, work through the following questions. Answer the last two questions only after engaging in conversation with the Lord. Your responses should result in specific steps to forge your path in the years ahead.

1. Your age when you first started your leadership journey:
2. Your current age:
3. Your intended retirement age:
4. Years of leadership remaining:
5. Years of leadership behind you:
6. What do you want your legacy to look like after the number of years you answered for #4?
7. What will it take to get you to #6?

increases in life expectancy, this season can last for several decades, into a woman's eighties and beyond. Although it is true that physical and mental capacities often decline during this stage, there is absolutely no reason that spiritual growth or ministry impact have to decline accordingly.

To the contrary, if a woman has completed the critical tasks of the preceding stages of life, the senior years can be a season of unparalleled influence and productivity. As Proverbs 20:29 points out, "The glory of young men is their strength, gray hair the splendor of the old." In his book *The Making of a Leader*, Robert Clinton calls this phase "Convergence." "Life Maturing and Ministry Maturing peak together during this period," he explains.[13] Some leaders even experience what Clinton calls "Celebration," a season during which "the fruit of a lifetime of ministry and growth culminates in an era of recognition and indirect influence on broad levels:

> Leaders in [Celebration] have built up a lifetime of contacts and continue to exert influence in these relationships. Others will seek them out because of their consistent track record in following God. Their storehouse of wisdom gathered over a lifetime of leadership will continue to bless and benefit many."[14]

KEY TASKS FOR CALLING IN THE SENIOR YEARS

The first key task in this life stage is to keep serving! God can use you until your very last breath. Aging is biblical (see Ecclesiastes 12:2-7 for a graphic and somewhat depressing description of the vagaries of old age!), but retirement is not, at least not in the sense of stepping away from all work and ministry in order to live for oneself. The type and amount of work might need to change, but the call and command to meaningful Kingdom impact is not age limited.

"That's the biggest surprise to me about getting older," writes author Patricia Raybon. "*God doesn't care about age. He needs willing workers. I used to think our best years were based on timing and talents. Both are important, to be sure. But our best years, it turns out, are based on our godly purpose—and our willingness to labor for the cause of it.*"[15]

The second key task is to finish well. It is never too late to make peace with your past, to mend broken relationships, to right past wrongs. If the time comes for you to step away from a formal ministry role, do your best to set up your successor for . . . well, success.

At age seventy-two, Dorothy is beginning what she describes as her fourth career, a ministry of writing and teaching. Before obeying her current calling, she worked as a speech pathologist, started and pastored a church, and taught at a Bible college, earning several advanced seminary degrees in the process.

"I have progressively come to the point now where I know that God has really deposited wisdom in me that I should leave behind," she said. "I belong to several groups that are very active in mentoring ministry. I think I am to reach back and be the Elizabeth to show other women the way, to help strengthen them in their journey."

If you are a "senior leader," I want you to know how much the church, and other women leaders in particular, need your voice, your experience, and your wisdom! You have walked a long and perhaps difficult path. As a professor of mine once said, "Somewhere, there is someone who wants to follow you." No matter your age—or more accurately, *because* of it—you have invaluable gifts to share. *Please* keep talking, serving, loving, and leading.

CALLING AND MOTHERHOOD

In addition to the age-based journey through life stages, many women also travel the parallel path of motherhood, which brings its own seasons or stages: from parenting littles (infants, toddlers, and preschool), to the school years, to the open- and empty-nest years. The parenting arc does not neatly correspond to a woman's age; for example, a woman in her midforties may be raising her own toddlers, or she may be an empty nester with several grandchildren. While different women have different perspectives on the relationship between motherhood and calling, the fact remains that motherhood and calling are inextricably connected. An understanding of calling affects a woman's perspective of motherhood, and the various stages of motherhood affect a woman's pursuit of her calling.

The Relationship between Motherhood and Calling

For some women, motherhood is and has always been their primary calling; for others, the call to motherhood is one of several or is not part of their calling at all. Raising children is a responsibility that takes tremendous time and attention, but there is no biblical teaching or example that a calling to the responsibility of motherhood automatically minimizes, negates, or replaces a calling to other ministry. Each woman must listen to the voice of the Spirit in this, considering the specifics of her own situation in light of the biblical principles of stewardship and accountability.

I am grieved when I hear stories from godly women who have experienced judgment (usually passive-aggressive, in the form of gossip and thinly veiled comments) about their choices on this issue. As with calling itself, there is no one-size-fits-all solution. Women can take any number of different but equally faithful and God-honoring approaches to motherhood and calling.

"I always felt this desire to be a wife and a mom," Amy told me. "As I got into my teenage years, I felt a lot of pressure from society to pick a career. When people ask what you want to be when you grow up, you sound silly when you say you want to be a wife and a mom and nothing else."

Married at age nineteen, Amy and her husband soon started a family, which now includes four biological children and one internationally adopted son. Amy leads a women's Bible study at her church, but her primary ministry is her immediate and extended family.

"My calling is still family, but it's bigger than my husband and children," Amy explained. "When my mom passed away when I was twenty-two, I became 'the person.' I help take care of my dad. When my sisters are hurting, they call me. It can be difficult, but my husband and I have both accepted that this is one of the ways God has called us."

Amy would not be surprised if her calling changes once her children leave the nest. "I don't know what it will be, but I'm definitely open to what will come later when I am not

CALLING AND SEASONS OF LIFE

needed at home full time," she said. "[Caring for family] is a lot right now, but that's not always how it's going to be."

Janette, on the other hand, combines motherhood with ministry outside the home as a full-time professor and part-time pastor. While juggling these roles comes at a cost, it's one that she and her husband—an emergency-room physician—are willing to pay.

"Most of my money goes to child care," Janette said. "To me, it's worth it, so that's an investment we make. I have a wonderful nanny. I am indebted to her for my career, and I am not ashamed of that. I couldn't do it without her—or my husband, of course. We both work. It's an investment in my calling that my family makes.

"I pinch myself that I get to do what I do," she continued. "I feel very fortunate that I have a partner who's supportive of it. But I also have to fight these inner voices: *Are you doing enough in this area?* When I'm at school, I'm thinking about my kids and dinner; when I'm making dinner, I'm thinking about my writing. I don't think I can avoid feelings of tension.

"At the same time, I know this is seasonal. Right now, I'm not going to publish as much as when my kids are out of the house. I have to make work fit around boundaries and borders. I am tired. I would like to go to sleep at a normal hour, but right now, when my kids are sleeping, I choose to work. It's all part of the good problem I have, of having too much to love. I get to do what I love—but I have a lot to love."

My experience falls between Amy's and Janette's. I received a clear call to occupational ministry when I was twenty-one years old. When I had my first child at age twenty-eight,

I didn't know how my new call to motherhood fit with my prior calling. Some folks in our church at the time assumed that parenthood supplanted any previous call. I never sensed that God had lifted my original calling, however.

At the same time, the reality was that motherhood, especially during that season, took a lot of my time and energy. I felt that if I did both motherhood and ministry full time, I would not do either of them well; therefore, I decided I would be a stay-at-home mom while my boys were young.

It wasn't easy; in fact, I think it contributed partly to the depression I experienced. I'm just not a "little-kid" person, plus I didn't have much community or outlet for my leadership gifts at our small, struggling church. But I felt strongly that I should be the primary caregiver and influence for my children at that stage in their lives, and I have never regretted my decision to stay home.

Once my boys grew old enough to enter school, I had more time to reengage in ministry leadership in my local church and beyond. I also earned my PhD, studying while my sons were in school or after they went to bed.

In those difficult early years, as I wrestled with the tension of two seemingly conflicting calls, God showed me that my work as a parent actually *was* fulfilling my ministry calling. Of course, my family was my primary ministry in terms of time and energy in that season. But motherhood actually fell under the umbrella of the God-given calling I have felt on my life since my twenties: to identify, develop, and encourage ministry leaders. I hadn't been released of that call; I was just doing it in a much more personal, intensive setting with my own children!

Again, these examples are descriptive, not prescriptive. There is no one "right" or "biblical" perspective or path. The best choice for one woman and her family will not be the best choice for another. A family's needs, a woman's personality and gifts, a spouse's perspective—all of these and many more factors must be considered in any decision. Remember, however, that some of your best leadership might happen behind the scenes, in your own home.

Seasons of the Parenting Journey

Each season of parenthood brings unique challenges and opportunities to the calling journey. There are three general seasons of parenting: the preschool years, the school years, and the open/empty-nest years. These seasons combine with general life stages to affect a woman's calling.

THE PRESCHOOL YEARS

This season begins with birth and continues through toddlerhood and preschool until a child begins elementary school at about age five. It is usually by far the most demanding stage in terms of time and energy. It is also often the stage in which women feel the most tension regarding their calling, as they decide how—or whether—to integrate ministry with the new demands of motherhood.

Pam, age thirty-five, is parenting three boys under the age of three while she also serves businesses and churches as a change-management consultant.

"When I was first a mom, I was determined to have it all. But trying to have it all was costing me my health and my life, and it just wasn't worth it," she said, her voice cracking with emotion. "I had to reframe my life to have the right 'all.' I became laser sharp on the things that were really important to me and accepted that this is a new season. It has its own beauty and sacrifices."

Ashley, a thirty-year-old pastor and mother of a toddler with a baby on the way, grew similarly emotional as she described her decision to step away from occupational ministry after the birth of her next child.

"I feel like I've been called to ministry. And I feel like I've been called to be a mom, and I've made a covenant with my husband and my child to raise her and nurture her. And in this season of life, I can't do both," she explained.

"It has been really confusing to me," Ashley confessed. "I feel sad, and I feel sure at the same time about my decision to step away. I've heard, 'Women can't do it all,' and I've spent so much time fighting that, saying, 'Yes, we can!' And now, being a woman who says I *can't* do it all . . . it's been really humbling." Ashley concluded tearfully, "Motherhood has rocked my world."

The first years of motherhood often bring women their first true experience of their limitations. It's a hard realization, accompanied by hard choices. The consolation is that while this season isn't easy, all women eventually find a way through it, becoming stronger, more self-aware—and often, more clear about their calling—in the process.

THE SCHOOL YEARS

This season begins at approximately age five and continues through graduation from high school at about age eighteen. During this stage, most families grow increasingly busy with school (or homeschool), church, and extracurricular activities, as kids find their own friends and interests. This activity peaks in high school, especially before a teen is old enough to drive.

I liken the start of the high-school years to the apex of a roller-coaster ride. For about fourteen years, parenting can feel like a slow but pleasant climb. While the ride is enjoyable, you begin to wonder if you will ever reach the top. Suddenly (or so it seems), you find yourself at the most scenic vista. You see how far you've come. You try to take in the view, you want to enjoy it a bit longer, but then—WHOOSH—you are whisked through a breathtaking series of loops, twists, and turns, some exhilarating and some nausea-inducing, until before you know it, you are coasting to the platform. You brake to a stop, fumble with your seat belt, and stagger out of the car and down the steps, wondering what just hit you.

Pursuing a ministry calling outside of motherhood during this season requires a good deal of strategic planning and logistical aptitude, but it is possible and perhaps even advisable, as we will see a little later in this chapter. It's also important to remember that there is no substitute for time with your children during these critical years.

"Honestly, I feel like I stepped back into ministry too quickly," reflected Sherry, now fifty-five. "That season of having kids at home—that never comes again. I wish I would have slowed down more. I wish I would have taken more time with my kids.

"As women, if God is calling us to something, we need to trust that he will align it with our season of life," she continued. "The ministry opportunities will come again. If you are really called to something, those opportunities will come to you again. The one door that will absolutely close is the time with your kids."

THE OPEN/EMPTY NEST

This season begins in late high school and continues into a child's adulthood. Although the traditional term for this has been the "empty nest," today the truly *empty* nest is preceded by an *open* nest, during which young-adult children fly in and out for as long as a decade. Even if adult children are present in the home, they require far less parental time and energy, freeing mothers to resume or ramp up external ministry or even to answer a new calling entirely.

Denise, Elizabeth, and Nancy all felt a new stirring in their hearts once their young-adult children left the nest. "I just feel like something new is coming," said Elizabeth, who was exploring ministry to women impacted by sex trafficking. Denise expressed similar sentiment after her oldest son graduated from high school and joined the air force: "I feel like God is preparing me for something." Nancy started teaching English as a Second Language to Burmese refugees in addition to her work as director at a church preschool.

Their experiences are not uncommon. Once their children have moved on to college, work, or the military, mothers once again have the time and space to consider what God is calling them toward in the next season of life. Women in this season may also experience greater financial and geographic flexibility.

"It pleases me to think that a woman raising children and organizing a family and a household is also storing up knowledge and questions, and then, at age forty-seven or fifty-two or fifty-six, there is *time*, and in the time, she can turn to a different kind of work. She can bloom a new and different flower, midway through her life," writes Lauren Winner.[16] In many ways, this season of parenting mirrors the life stage of young adulthood: The future may once again be wide open, this time with the benefit of decades of life of experience and wisdom.

How Calling Affects Children

We have explored the many ways that having children can affect our calling. But what about how calling affects our children?

One of my all-time favorite parenting memories is of my doctoral-dissertation hearing, which my husband and both of our boys, then ages ten and twelve, attended. My boys knew that for years, I had spent a lot of time in my office and at the local university library, working on some big paper that used the word *leadership* a lot. They sat through what I'm sure was to them a very boring presentation and Q&A about my research with my faculty committee, which then dismissed the four of us to the hall while they deliberated my fate.

A few minutes later, we were summoned back into the classroom, where my supervising professor uttered the words I had worked toward for the past five years: "Congratulations, Doctor!" I will never forget my sons' expressions at that moment. Their eyes lit up with excitement, and their faces were full of pride as they ran over to hug me.

I suddenly realized that my greatest achievement was not

my PhD; it was what my boys had learned in the process. They saw that their mom had her own life and important work. They saw that their dad was fully supportive in both word and deed. They learned about Kingdom, ministry, leadership, and calling from the example we set as parents. And in the process of working toward a PhD to enable me to better develop ministry leaders for the church, I developed the two young leaders in my home.

In addition to seeing you engaged in Kingdom work, kids can grow from honest conversations about your calling and the challenges you have experienced on that journey. "Your children *are* watching what you live out, and they will learn your ministry values if you involve them and talk about your decisions with them," advised Polly, sixty-three. "They will someday surprise you with leadership skills of their own—and sooner than you might imagine. Stay the course!"

Sometimes, obedience to your or your husband's calling may bring significant change to your child's world. For example, your family may need to move to a new church or community. Moves like this can rock a child's world. There is no easy path in these situations. Some families decide they can wait until a natural transition point for their kids (for example, the summer before starting middle or high school), while others may not feel they have a choice.

Whatever your situation, seek to communicate your values and engage your children in the decision as best you can for their level of understanding. The change may be very difficult, but it can also be a tremendous learning and bonding experience for all of you. (One caveat: If you are going to deliver hard news, don't always do it at the same restaurant.

To this day, our boys still get suspicious when we suggest a trip to Cold Stone Creamery for ice cream!)

At the same time, remember that what feels so important to you in your ministry may not be on your child's mind at all. "No doubt the most challenging day I had in juggling the mom-in-ministry role was on 9/11," recalled Fran, who was a pastor the day of the tragic terrorist attacks.

"Our church staff immediately set about collecting resources, gathering lay counselors, and preparing a service for that evening," Fran recounted. "But when I picked up my girls from school, it wasn't the tragedy in New York that most concerned them. It was the fate of our guinea pig, who had major surgery that day. Their questions weren't about terrorism and national security; they were more along the lines of would the pig make it through the night and, 'Mommy, do you really have to go out tonight?'"

WHAT NOW?

As we seek to faithfully obey our calling through every season of life and parenting, let's keep a couple key principles in mind.

First, *embrace each season*. Life consists of seasons. No matter how beautiful or difficult a season, it will not last forever. Commit to embracing each season as you experience it. Be fully present, instead of looking behind or ahead. And don't compare your experience. Your seasons are unique to you and will not align with anyone else's.

Second, *embrace the tension*. Pastor Andy Stanley says that we often view challenges as problems to be solved rather than as tensions to be managed.[17] Don't expect calling and season of life to always fit neatly together. At every stage of your life and parenting journey, you will experience questions and points of tension in relation to your calling. Accept and even embrace them as opportunities to draw closer to God and to grow in maturity and relationship with him.

CONTINUE THE CONVERSATION

» What season of life and parenting are you in currently? What "great questions" are you asking in this season?

» What "tensions" do you feel most acutely at this time?

» In what stage of "the critical journey" would you place yourself?

» What are the key tasks for your current season of life, and how specifically will you navigate them?

» What are you modeling to your children about calling, leadership, and ministry?

Chapter 6

CALLING AND MONEY

I vividly remember the first job offer my husband received over twenty years ago. "The Elder Board voted unanimously to call you to the position of Associate Pastor," the letter read. "Your salary will be $33,500, including benefits."

As two young newlyweds just out of seminary, we felt like we had just won the lottery. A church was going to *pay* us—thousands of dollars! on a regular basis!—for the opportunity to be in ministry? I'm sure we celebrated by ordering the *large* fries at McDonald's.

Of course, after factoring in Social Security, taxes, tithe, health insurance, decent housing in our major metropolitan area, insurance, food, entertainment, transportation, student-loan debt, and small contributions to savings and retirement accounts, suddenly the large fries seemed a bit extravagant.

We didn't go into ministry for the money, and so far that's worked out really well for us.

Still, although finances have sometimes been tight (and sometimes *very* tight), we have never gone hungry. We have always had a roof over our heads and for the most part stayed warm during the Minnesota winters and cool during the North Carolina summers. We fed and clothed and transported and extracurricular-ed two boys for eighteen years each. (Thankfully, what we paid for their car-insurance premiums we will hopefully save in wedding expenses.)

It is a fact of modern life that money makes the world go 'round. Despite attempts by some to live without money,[1] the majority of us need at least a modicum of it to survive. What, then, is the relationship between money and calling? How does money—either a lack of it or an abundance of it—affect the pursuit of your calling? Where is the line between stepping out in faith and acting in foolishness? And how do the biblical commands, examples, and principles about money apply specifically to *your* calling and current situation?

MONEY IN SCRIPTURE

The Bible talks more about money than about any other topic: There are over two thousand references, including more than nine hundred regarding personal finance. But the Bible rarely speaks directly about the relationship between money and a Christian's specific, secondary calling. As we examine biblical commands, principles, and examples about money in general, we can glean insight about how to handle money within our calling.

Where the Bible lists direct commands about money, the dominant theme is one of relationship: both our relationship to money and how we use money in relationship to others. Regarding our relationship to money, King David instructs us to not "set our heart" on it, even if riches increase (Psalm 62:10), while Proverbs exhorts, "Don't wear yourself out trying to get rich" (Proverbs 23:4, NLT). In Matthew, Jesus teaches his followers to lay up treasures in heaven instead of on earth, where moth and rust can destroy (Matthew 6:19-20).

Regarding money in relationship to others, the Bible speaks clearly to three areas of relationship: with God, with human authority, and with other human beings. Believers are to trust in God, not in money (1 Timothy 6:17). The Lord also commands Christians to pay what is owed to government authorities (Matthew 22:21; Romans 13:1, 6-7), to give generously to those in need (Proverbs 3:27; Matthew 5:42; Luke 6:35; 12:33; 2 Corinthians 8:7), to not steal or cheat anyone (Exodus 20:15; Leviticus 19:13; Mark 10:19; Luke 3:12-14), to never oppress the poor with high interest rates (Proverbs 28:8), and to not be burdened by outstanding debt (Romans 13:8).

From the abundance of biblical teaching regarding money, there emerge several dominant principles: responsibility, contentment, generosity, the temporal nature of money, and the promise of God's provision. Working backward from this list, let's take a look at what the Bible says about each of these key themes.

- **The Promise of God's Provision.** There is no question that God has the ability and desire to provide for his children. The Bible tells us that God owns "the cattle on a thousand hills" (Psalm 50:10), and that he will provide for all our needs (Psalm 107:9; Proverbs 10:3; Luke 12:27-31; Philippians 4:19).

- **The Temporal Nature of Money.** Money is fleeting—here today and gone tomorrow—and never fully satisfies. "Cast but a glance at riches, and they are gone," Proverbs says, "for they will surely sprout wings and fly off to the sky like an eagle" (Proverbs 23:5). This principle is stated even more directly in one of my all-time favorite verses: "Trust in your money and down you go!" (Proverbs 11:28, NLT). The writer of these proverbs—King Solomon, at that time the wealthiest man in the world—continued his pessimistic observations in the book of Ecclesiastes:

> Whoever loves money never has enough;
> whoever loves wealth is never satisfied
>   with their income.
> This too is meaningless.
>
> As goods increase,
> so do those who consume them.
> And what benefit are they to the owners
> except to feast their eyes on them? . . .
>
> Everyone comes naked from their mother's womb,
> and as everyone comes, so they depart.
> They take nothing from their toil
> that they can carry in their hands.
>
> ECCLESIASTES 5:10-11, 15

Paul concurred in his first letter to Timothy, writing, "We brought nothing into the world, and we can take nothing out of it" (1 Timothy 6:7).

- **Generosity.** As we have noted earlier, the Bible repeatedly commands Christ followers to give generously to those in need, without expectation of repayment (Psalm 37:21; Luke 6:35). The New Testament teaches that Christians should give quietly (Matthew 6:2-4), habitually (1 Corinthians 16:2), proportionately (Deuteronomy 16:17), intentionally (2 Corinthians 9:7), willingly (Proverbs 21:26), cheerfully (2 Corinthians 9:7), sacrificially (2 Corinthians 8:1-5), with love (1 Corinthians 13:3), and as an act of worship (Philippians 4:18).

- **Contentment.** The Bible exhorts believers to be satisfied with what they have been given. "Better a little with the fear of the LORD than great wealth with turmoil," Proverbs states (Proverbs 15:16). Jesus taught his followers to store up treasures in heaven rather than on earth (Matthew 6:19-21) and that it is far better to lose the world but gain one's soul (Matthew 16:26). Paul attested that God's power works best in our weakness (2 Corinthians 12:9-10) and that he had learned to be content both in plenty and in need (Philippians 4:11-12). And in his first letter to Timothy, Paul wrote that "godliness with contentment is great gain" and that "the love of money is a root of all kinds of evil" (1 Timothy 6:6, 10).

- **Responsibility.** The Bible champions responsibility in a variety of areas of life related to money. Employers are responsible to provide fair wages for workers (Leviticus 19:13; Luke 10:7; 1 Timothy 5:18). Borrowers are responsible to repay outstanding debt (Psalm 37:21; Proverbs 22:7; Romans 13:7). Parents and grandparents are responsible to provide for their households and extended family (Proverbs 13:22; 1 Timothy 5:8). The wise demonstrate responsibility by counting the cost of a project (Luke 14:28-30) and taking precautions against danger (Proverbs 27:12). Each of these responsibilities flow from the guiding principle of stewardship that runs throughout Scripture.

The Bible provides several instructive examples of the relationship between money and people involved in ministry service. For starters, we learn in the book of Numbers that the Levites—the tribe who were designated for priestly service to the nation of Israel—did not receive an inheritance of property in the Promised Land, further setting them apart from the other eleven tribes (Numbers 18:20). "Instead, [the Levites] were to look to God alone for their day-to-day sustenance and long-term security," writes Steve Shadrach.[2]

Part of God's provision came in the form of an allowance for the priests to eat the leftovers of the food offerings they presented to the Lord on behalf of the Israelites. This food was considered payment for the Levites' work (Numbers 18:31), setting the precedent that workers in the Lord's service are worthy of material compensation.

The Gospels note several intersections between money

and Jesus' ministry. Matthew tells us that when Jesus asked Peter and Andrew and then James and John to follow him to become fishers of men, they left their nets—not just that day's fishing, but their very *livelihood*—without hesitation ("at once"; "immediately") to join him (Matthew 4:18-22). We also know that this ministry required money: Many women contributed personal financial support to Jesus and the disciples (Luke 8:3), while Judas served as the operation's treasurer (John 12:6; 13:29), albeit a corrupt one. When Jesus sent out the twelve and then the seventy-two, he instructed them not to take food but to rely only on the hospitality offered to them on their travels.

We also see how wealth impacted a person's desire or ability to follow Christ. When Jesus told a rich young ruler to sell his possessions and give them to the poor, the young man "went away sad, because he had great wealth" (Matthew 19:22; Mark 10:22). On the other hand, Zacchaeus the tax collector was so motivated to follow Jesus that he gave half of his possessions to the poor and vowed to pay back anybody he had cheated, at four times the original amount (Luke 19:1-10).

From the earliest days of the church, believers shared their possessions and contributed financial resources in support of local and missionary ministry (Acts 2:44-45).[3] Meanwhile, although the apostle Paul sometimes relied on the hospitality of others during his travels and defended his right to receive compensation for his ministry, he often chose to forgo that right in order to preach the gospel without restriction, supporting himself financially through his work as a tentmaker (Acts 18:1-3; 1 Corinthians 9:1-18). God promises to provide all our needs, but that leaves a lot of leeway as to what will be provided and how it will be provided as we follow our calling.

MONEY AND MINISTRY

I've realized over the years that money really complicates ministry. And it's not just the diffculty of talking about money in an organization—the stuff of sermons and stewardship campaigns. Salaries and budget shortfalls. That's really the easy stuff.

What about a leader's personal relationship with money?

I am a ministry leader and a pastor's wife. While I earn money through my writing and teaching, the bulk of our family's income comes from my husband's salary, paid for by our church. It has always been this way for us, nearly thirty years in full-time employment by one church or another.

I am accustomed to making our living through the church. Yet I continue to be troubled by the potential traps and trappings of this arrangement.

Sometimes I am aware that the people in our church watch what we do with our money. Most of the time, I don't feel that they intentionally scrutinize. This is probably partly because we don't live extravagantly, and partly because a certain standard of living has always been assumed in the communities where we have lived and ministered. If we don't push the boundaries on either end of this standard, no one bats an eye.

Each of us makes choices about money that speak loudly to the people around us. What we do with our money communicates our values, our priorities, our theology. Our lifestyle is a teaching tool. The way we use money can negate what we say we believe or it can foster conversations and challenges that no stewardship lesson can match.

What does our relationship with money, and the possessions and experiences it buys, communicate to the people with whom we work and worship?

What do we communicate if our house is one of the nicest among those we serve and lead? What if it is one of the smallest? Would Jesus drive a BMW? Should we? Is a new Camry okay? What about a gas-guzzling SUV?

How should we as leaders live *in* our culture but not *of* it when it comes to money?

We are called to live among the people in our community. Yet we are also called to be set apart as a follower of Christ and to not conform to the patterns of this world. Do we go along with the culture of our community and sign up our kids for all manner of lessons and camps, or do we forgo some of those experiences in order to give more to the poor and needy in our community and around the world? Should we prioritize involvement in activities with those in our community, or the needs of those we have never met? What do those decisions communicate to our friends, neighbors, and church family?

And those are just questions of lifestyle. What about how money colors our leadership?

Are we afraid to speak hard truth because the givers or donors might leave? I've seen it happen too many times: Church leadership becomes hesitant to go this way or that, speak this thing or that, because of how the "heavy hitters" might respond. We can be tempted to acquiesce in the face of this pressure.

Do we lead differently because we know this organization pays our salary and therefore our family's bills? On the flip side, do we experience or express entitlement regarding salary and benefits, believing that the organization "owes" us something? What if money weren't an issue and we were financially independent? How might we lead or speak differently?

I'll admit that I have many more questions than answers. My husband and I continue to pray for wisdom and direction in these areas, learning as we grow. We have chosen a smaller, simpler house and fewer possessions. Sometimes we decline opportunities for ourselves and for our children in order to give that money to other needs. We have learned to redefine needs and to distinguish between true needs and personal wants. And I dream that our family will one day be financially independent of our church, or in a position that we can "reverse tithe," giving back to the churches that have given so much to us over the years.

Those are decisions and dreams for our family; they are descriptive, not prescriptive. I know that my answers will be different from those of anyone else. But I believe that each ministry leader, couple, and family must at least wrestle with these questions.[4] As we consider the role money plays in our ministry and calling, there are a few guiding principles that can help us discern our way forward.

1. Money Is Important

Money is a dominant topic in Scripture, and it is no less important today. We need at least some of it to operate and to pursue or support our calling in our contemporary world. I would suggest two related truths as we consider money's place in our lives and calling: First, *many of us probably need less money than we think*. Second, *God can provide more than we imagine*. As missionary Hudson Taylor declared, "God's work done in God's way will never lack God's supply." It is more important to focus on our relationship to money—and on how it affects our other relationships—than on how much of it we possess.

2. Money Complicates Relationships

Money has the potential to complicate our relationship with God and with others. The Bible is clear that no one can serve both God and money (Luke 16:13) and that the lure of wealth can choke the seed of the gospel (Mark 4:19; Luke 8:14), lead people away from the faith (1 Timothy 6:10), and impede discipleship (Mark 10:23-27). The Bible also teaches that the borrower is a slave to the lender, creating an unbalanced power dynamic (1 Peter 5:2-3). In addition, asking and relying on others for financial support of a ministry can change the dynamics of personal relationships. Finally, money can complicate ministry itself, affecting both lifestyle and leadership.

3. Money Can Be a Tool or a Burden

Money can certainly be a blessing to the pursuit of one's calling. It can pay for education, for living expenses, and for the costs of the actual work of ministry. But money can also be a hindrance to pursuing our calling, and not just when we don't have enough of it. Both debt and wealth can keep believers from obeying God's calling.

DEBT

According to the United States Federal Reserve, the average American household carries over $137,000 in combined debt. The average debt on student loans, for those who have them, is around $50,000, while families with credit-card and auto-loan debt carry additional average balances of nearly $17,000 and $30,000, respectively.[5] Remember the Bible's teaching that the borrower is a slave to the lender? The numbers above represent a whole lot of financial bondage.

Seminary graduates may be even more challenged, as the debt for their theological education outpaces their potential earning power. As of 2018, the average student-loan debt for seminary graduates was $36,000.[6] However, many churches still prefer a seminary graduate, especially for pastoral positions, and many students feel that theological training is completely out of reach without loan assistance.

While it is not un-Christian to take out a loan for education, housing, or transportation expenses, it is essential to go into any type of debt agreement with eyes wide open and only after much deliberation, wise counsel, and prayer. Debt is a responsibility assumed and places the borrower in financial bondage. Weigh the long-term cost of repayment against any perceived short-term advantages. For example, Kara and her husband believe that God may be calling them to overseas mission work. They are not yet able to act on that calling, however, as they are both working to repay tens of thousands of dollars in student loans.

While loans may seem to be God's provision, the Bible does not say that it is wise to borrow, that God will bail a person out of debt, or that debt is an exercise in faith. "To say that we're exercising faith by borrowing money is the same as saying that God needs to use a lender to meet our needs," Focus on the Family points out.[7]

In addition, the book of James cautions against making commitments based only on future speculation. "Now listen, you who say, 'Today or tomorrow we will go to this or that city, spend a year there, carry on business and make money,'" James writes. "Why, you do not even know what will happen tomorrow. What is your life? You are a mist that appears for a little while and then vanishes. Instead, you ought to say, 'If it is the Lord's will, we will live and do this or that'" (James 4:13-15).

My husband and I learned the hard reality of this passage about a dozen years into our marriage, when we bought a larger house and assumed a bigger mortgage with a longer-term loan, all on the promise of a raise. We thought we would stretch our budget for a year before the raise kicked in. Instead, the global economy collapsed. (Anybody else remember 2008?) Instead of receiving a raise, we took a pay cut, lost several years of retirement contributions by the church, and faced higher expenses for everything from groceries to gasoline. To make matters worse, what we thought was our dream house had more problems and expensive repairs than any of our homes before or since. The housing market collapsed with the recession, and we had to rent and then sell the home at a huge loss after a move for ministry. It took nearly ten years to make a full financial recovery.

WEALTH

Sometimes the barrier to following God's calling isn't lack of money but rather an abundance of it. We have already seen how money can complicate our relationship with God. It changes our perspective and our priorities. The great preacher John Wesley believed that wealth was one of the greatest threats to the effectiveness of Christianity.[8] Leading by example, he fought against "lifestyle inflation" and lived his entire life on the same income as he had as a college student, giving away the rest. "Money never stays with me," Wesley reportedly said. "I throw it out of my hands as soon as possible, lest it should find its way into my heart."[9]

The 1994 movie *Quiz Show* tells the story of Charles Van Doren, the scion of a well-known New England literary family who became infamous for his participation in a television quiz-show scandal in the 1950s. The movie depicts a scene in which a lawyer interrogates Van Doren about his motives for cheating. "Was it just the money, Charlie?" the attorney asks. Van Doren replies, "You'll forgive me, but anyone who thinks money is ever 'just money' couldn't have much of it."[10] The more money we have, the more important money becomes, and the harder it is to give it up and to make clear decisions related to it.

When it comes to money, we would all be wise to echo the plea of the writer in Proverbs: "Give me neither poverty nor riches! Give me just enough to satisfy my needs. For if I grow rich, I may deny you and say, 'Who is the LORD?' And if I am too poor, I may steal and thus insult God's holy name" (Proverbs 30:8-9, NLT).

4. Calling Requires Sacrifice

Despite what some television preachers may tell you, the Bible never promises wealth to those who follow Christ. In fact, following any call from the Lord requires sacrifice: a willingness to submit ourselves and our desires and to potentially give up our financial resources, comfort, and security.

"Calling means that, for the follower of Christ, there is a decisive, immediate, and moment-by-moment authority above money and the market," writes Os Guinness. "Thus there are, if you like, two economies—a 'calling economy' as well as a 'commercial economy'—and for followers of Christ the former, not the latter, is supreme."[11]

Jesus' original disciples made significant sacrifices to follow Christ, and believers today must also expect to make sacrifices, although those sacrifices will look different for each person. It may mean fewer lattes each week. It may mean moving to a smaller house or paying the added expense for a bigger one. It may mean leaving a job or taking on another. It may mean driving an older car, sticking with an older phone, or dropping cable. "Yesterday's luxuries need not always become today's necessities even if everyone around us acquires them," Craig Blomberg wisely notes in his immensely thorough and practical book, *Christians in an Age of Wealth.*[12]

For LeeAnn and her husband, the decision to adopt two international children with physical needs had a number of financial ramifications. "We dropped $30,000 on travel and adoption for our first child and then $28,000 for our second child nine months later," she recalled. "None of that was planned and saved for but we felt like it was something that was too important to pass over. You're looking at kids with special needs; that costs money and takes away from retirement savings, from college funds, from all these goals you have set. But for us, it was just part of the package. We knew we needed to do it."

LeeAnn became very aware of the constant temptation to compare her family's financial situation to others. "It's ridiculous what Satan can do to your mind, telling you to compare yourself to others," she continued. "But once I knew of hundreds of thousands of kids with medical issues who need to be adopted, it was hard to say, 'I want to go on nice vacations.'"

Pam had a clear sense that God was calling her to use her experience in corporate change management to help churches grow. Following that calling would require her to give up her current job and six-figure income in one of the most expensive cities in the country. As she and her husband prayed about options, they felt the answer was to move their family to a less expensive part of the country, where they could live sustainably on one income and allow Pam to invest her time helping churches.

Within months, Pam left her corporate position, her husband found a new job, the couple sold their house, and their family of five moved six hundred miles to a smaller city in the southeastern United States. "We moved down here with me literally leaving a six-figure salary, teaching opportunities at a nearby college, and family up north," Pam said. "On paper, it's foolish. It makes no sense. Yet it makes all the sense in the world.

"I remember distinctly when God called me to grow the church, and I distinctly remember when he said, 'If you take care of my church, I will take care of your family,'" she continued. "That's not to say there haven't been moments when this one-income thing really stinks. We have had to make changes to our lifestyle and really put our faith in God. There is no doubt that I am doing what I'm called to do. The Lord surpasses our expectations."

5. Biblical Principles Must Take Precedence

In matters of money pertaining to personal calling, biblical principles—including responsibility, contentment, generosity, the temporal nature of money, and the promise of God's provision—always apply. Moreover, we must hew to God's understanding and definition of these principles, not to those of our culture, which have likely seeped into our churches, as well. For example, Christians have a biblical responsibility to provide for family members. But what does that mean? Food and shelter, yes, but what else? God promises to provide for our needs, but what constitutes a genuine need? A fully-funded 529 college savings account? Annual destination vacations? We need to ruthlessly evaluate our values and behaviors in light of biblical principles and be willing to give up any of our riches if they stand in the way of our obedience to his calling or our ability to hear it in the first place.

Jillian was thirty years old with a three-year-old and a baby on the way when she and her husband left their current church to plant a new one. "We started the church with absolutely no backing whatsoever," she recalled. "We had no ministry backing, no financial backing, no mentor to support us. We were just kind of figuring things out as we went. My husband had studied and read books and attended conferences, so he felt like he was prepared. But I had absolutely no idea what the heck we were doing."

To make ends meet, Jillian's husband worked full time as a contractor, running his own business for about five years while starting the church. "It was rather intense, and thank goodness we were young," she said. "My husband finally went to our core group and said the only way they could make this work was if he stopped working two jobs and focused on building the church.

"It was the scariest thing we've ever done," Jillian continued. "There was no promise of money or any salary; the core group just said, 'We'll do what we can.' We went probably three to four years of really, really having money problems. Many times, we would get shutoff notices for our own utilities. Many times, we would just get by with five bucks.

"I remember one day, we were just broke. We didn't have a lot of food in our refrigerator. We had one roll of toilet paper left, and I wondered what would happen when we ran out of toilet paper. We went to my in-laws that Sunday, honestly hoping they would feed us. They did bless us with a little bit of money, but that money runs out really quick when your bills are overdue and you have babies.

"I was doing laundry later that week," Jillian recalled. "I had pulled all my clothes out of the dryer and there was this shredded thing at the end of my clothes. I took a closer look and realized it was my very last five dollars. I fell to my knees, hysterical. I felt so desperate, I just bawled. I couldn't get over the fact that God would let that happen to my last five dollars. But now I still keep a piece of that five-dollar bill on my dryer to remind me how faithful God is. It wasn't long after that when our church doubled in size, our church finances doubled, we were able to take a salary, to pay our bills, even to be able to bless others. I can look back at that little piece of a five-dollar bill and remember that feeling of desperation but also remember how God has been faithful, even though I couldn't see the clearing at all."

Would Jillian recommend their path to others?

"I struggle with an answer because we would not be the stewards we are now if we didn't struggle," she said. "I wouldn't recommend jumping out of a boat with no sort of financial backing. It is a terrible, difficult path. But at the same time, I recognize what it did for us, and how God loved us and made us who we are because we struggled the way we did. I feel like God needed us to be desperate, to have complete faith in what he wanted us to do. The moment we feel that we have a handle on finances is the moment we forget God was the giver of all that."

ANSWERING A CALL WHEN MONEY TALKS

Assuming you have put money in its rightful place in your life and are managing your financial responsibilities, such as family provision and debt repayment, what are your options for meeting monetary need when obeying a calling? I believe there are at least five potential solutions.

The first option is to pursue opportunities that require no money, or at least no additional money. This could mean volunteering. It could also mean taking a job that pays you (although perhaps not lucratively) for following your calling.

The second option is to borrow money. As we have explored earlier, however, debt is very dangerous. Before going down that road, be sure to explore all other options.

Recognize that you are putting yourself in a form of bondage by assuming debt, even for a worthy purpose such as additional education.

The third option is to use your own money to cover expenses involved with following your calling. Perhaps a spouse can serve as the primary breadwinner. "If my husband didn't have a good, secure, well-paying job, I couldn't fulfill my calling," said Denise, a mother of two who works part time as the middle-school ministry director at a local church. Or perhaps your family has enough financial resources to cover necessary costs. Again, the less debt you have and the less money you need to live on, the more resources you have for opportunities that God may present.

A fourth option is to ask others for money, either in the form of a gift from family or friends or in contributions to a charitable organization that then provides a salary for the ministry employee. The latter path is typically utilized by parachurch nonprofits such as campus ministries and overseas-missions agencies. This approach allows others to be involved in ministry via their financial support. It also builds the faith of the individual asking for that support.

That approach was just fine for Elizabeth, who, with her husband, raised financial support for their missionary work in Ireland and the Philippines. "For us, regarding support raising, we've always believed that if God is calling us to ministry, he's going to provide for us in this way because this is how he has provided through our missions organization for many, many years," she said. "That doesn't mean it was easy to do, but we knew that was what God wanted us to do, so we had no qualms about raising the support."

A fifth option is to wait to fully pursue your calling. During that waiting period, you might keep working or begin saving. You might also discover ways to take baby steps toward your calling instead of making one big leap.

Andrea decided that she needed to pay off her student loans before moving to Nicaragua as a missionary. "I didn't want to go into full-time ministry and raise support if I was still in debt with car and student loans," she explained. "I didn't want to feel like I was asking people to support my college fund." By working at a low-income school for five years after college, Andrea qualified for student-loan forgiveness and paid off her remaining debt. Meanwhile, she volunteered in the youth ministry at her local church and took several short-term trips to the country that is now her ministry home.

The final option is to take a leap of faith and trust God to provide. Indeed, according to Os Guinness, "Holy folly is central to the call to discipleship,"[13] and believers are often called to be obedient without knowing final outcomes. Dallas Willard points out, however, that faith is not actually a "wild, desperate 'leap'"—it is "confidence grounded in reality."[14] In other words, when believers orient their lives around God's principles, a leap is not really a blind jump but rather the clear next step, taken with full confidence based on faithfulness already experienced.

Jill had been feeling God's clear calling to leave her full-time job at a large church in order to be more present to her teenage children during a difficult season at home. But she battled fears about financial provision and her self-worth. "There was something prideful for me to be able to say, 'I do full-time ministry,'" Jill said. "Part of my identity was wrapped up in that. I fought staying home for weeks. But God very clearly said to me, 'You are going home on August 15.' So I said okay and turned in my resignation.

"I put in my resignation and was getting ready to go in to work on my last morning when my husband called me over to him. He said, 'I've got to tell you something. I totally missed this in my emails, but my company just put a huge bonus in my account that covers you being home for years and years.' It was just confirmation for me," Jill continued. "God was saying, *I've got you, you'll be okay.* He just carried us through that time."

Of the options above, the best one for you will depend on a number of factors that are unique to your own situation. As with any decision regarding God's calling, consideration regarding financial issues should incorporate honest conversation with the Lord and wise counsel from mature Christians.

WHAT NOW?

As you consider this conversation about money and calling, I would like to suggest two action steps that have the potential to redirect your entire life and ministry.

First, *evaluate your relationship to money.* Money is too important and influential—in both our physical world and our spiritual life—to not take its power and position seriously. Spend some time in honest reflection about the place money has been given in your life. Repent and reposition as needed.

WOMEN SPEAK: CALLING AND MONEY

What role has money played in the pursuit of your calling?

- "I felt like I couldn't entertain what my calling even *could* be until we were out of debt. Paying off my student loans was the first step in order to have control over our money and have the freedom to explore options."—*Kellie*

- "I'm doing what I want and feel called to do, but it's not as valued by my husband because it doesn't bring in the cash that his job does. It's a perception problem that affects things like getting a sitter or going to an evening meeting. He feels 'it's not worth it' because I'm not getting paid a lot."—*Kelly*

- "I feel as if perhaps my calling has made me rely more on my faith—faith that the finances will work themselves out, because I willingly don't work full time in a well-paying job for which I have trained, in order to pursue my calling."—*Stacey*

- "I work for a faith-based mission agency, which means our family is completely reliant on donations—but we never ask people to donate! Somehow, we have always been able to pay our bills, and God has met every need for all 1,400 missionaries in our agency!"—*Sarah*

Second, *always play by God's rules*. Orient your every financial decision around the biblical principles of responsibility, contentment, generosity, the temporal nature of money, and the promise of God's provision. Once your compass is set to true north regarding money, answers to your questions about your specific calling and next steps will likely become clearer.

CONTINUE THE CONVERSATION

» In what ways are you burdened by money, either by debt or by wealth?

» Which of the biblical principles about money are most challenging to you, and in what ways?

» Have you experienced complications in your relationships with God, with others, or in your ministry because of money?

» In what ways have you made financial sacrifices to be obedient to your calling? Is God calling you to any other sacrifices at this time?

» Where have you seen God's provision in unexpected ways in your life and ministry?

Chapter 7

CALLING AND CHALLENGES

This was not how things were supposed to work out.

Every night for a year, my husband and I had prayed that God would direct us to the right place in his right timing. Based on our own prayers as well as confirmation from others, it seemed that the "right place" would be a church where Dave could serve as senior pastor, giving him more opportunities to exercise his gifts of preaching and shepherding. Now that we had two little boys, we also desired to be closer to family. We told God that we would go anywhere he led us (and we meant it!), but that we would love to end up somewhere in the southeastern United States, ideally within three hours of Dave's parents.

We explored options around the country. We prayed, waited, and sought counsel from wise and mature believers.

We continued to serve faithfully in our current ministries. We prayed and waited some more.

Twelve months later, our little family made the 1,200-mile journey from Minnesota to our new church in North Carolina—just two and a half hours from our sons' beloved Nana and Papa—where Dave would serve as lead pastor. We felt God had clearly answered our earnest prayers, as evidenced by all sorts of confirmations that seemed like way more than coincidence. I mean, at the boarding gate for our flight home from our interview weekend, we discovered that our pilot "happened" to be a friend who first came up to Dave a year earlier and said he felt God was preparing my husband for a lead pastoral role!

We were over-the-moon excited. We felt we had come home, and we thought we'd be at that church and in that city for life.

Yet three years in, our dream situation had turned to a nightmare. Our church was slowly dying, our marriage was on the rocks, and I felt a searing isolation that would eventually lead to full-blown depression.

We left that church after five years and slowly began repairing the tears in our marriage, but our next church in a neighboring city provided only marginal ministry respite. Cultural dynamics and leadership transitions led to another painful departure after another five years. After a mutually beneficial nine-month interim ministry at a third church, we landed back in the Midwest, wondering what had gone wrong.

We thought we were seeking and obeying God, yet our time in North Carolina was by far our hardest season of ministry, marriage, and personal life. Had we not heard God correctly? Were we blinded by our own desires? Had we lost our ability to do ministry and make friendships?

Every follower of Christ will experience challenges on the calling journey. Some of these challenges are small speed bumps, while others may cause a leader to doubt her calling, her gifts, perhaps even her self-worth or her faith. In this chapter, we will explore what the Bible says about challenges, look at some of the most common types of challenges, and consider the potential responses to these challenges.

THE CHALLENGES OF CALLING

The Bible never promises that following God will be easy. In fact, Jesus says that believers should expect to experience trouble in this world (John 16:33). While this verse also promises that Christ will have ultimate victory, the Bible gives plenty of examples of men and women who experienced challenges as they sought to obey God's calling:

- Abraham was asked to trust God and say good-bye to his country and family without knowing his end destination (Genesis 12:1).
- Joseph languished in prison for years on false charges before God's purpose became clear and he became second in command in Egypt and led the country through an extended famine (Genesis 39–41).
- Moses spent forty years in desert exile before being tapped by God to lead the Hebrews out of Egypt, then spent the next forty years questioning God's

calling as he was constantly questioned and mocked by the people he was leading (Exodus).

- Esther risked her life to ask favor for the Jewish people from her husband, King Xerxes (Esther 4:15-16).
- The Old Testament prophets were subjected to ridicule, false accusations, outright rejection, physical threats, and actual violence (1 Samuel; 1 and 2 Kings; Ezra; Isaiah; Jeremiah; Amos; Micah).
- Jesus sent his disciples as "lambs among wolves" and warned that they may be rejected for sharing the gospel (Mark 6:7-11; Luke 10:1-12).
- The apostle Paul was often hungry, thirsty, and naked during the course of his ministry. He was whipped, beaten, shipwrecked, and threatened, and he felt a constant burden for those in his spiritual care (2 Corinthians 11:16-33).
- Paul, Silas, Peter, and John were repeatedly imprisoned (Acts 4, 12, 16).
- The apostle John was exiled and died on the island of Patmos (Revelation 1:9).
- Jesus himself was "despised and rejected," "a Man of sorrows and acquainted with grief" (Isaiah 53:3, NKJV).

In other words, following God involves hardship, especially when we are called to walk the often lonely road of leadership. The question is not *whether* we will experience challenges in the course of following our calling, but *what kind* of challenges we will experience and *how* we will respond to them. These experiences can be complicated by the authority and responsibility that come with a specific leadership role or title.

Challenges on the calling journey can originate either externally or internally. Sometimes, an external challenge may trigger an internal crisis, such as when criticism from another person causes us to question our calling. It would be impossible to provide an exhaustive list of challenges. But we will likely find ourselves facing a few common experiences as we pursue our calling.

Criticism

At some point (probably many!) on your journey as a leader, you will be criticized: either for your work or for who you are as a person; either publicly, privately, or when you are not present. No matter the reason or the source, criticism cuts deep because each of us has a fundamental desire to be loved, accepted, and respected just as we are.

Given that criticism is inevitable, we must learn how to handle it. "The key player is not the giver, but the receiver," note Douglas Stone and Sheila Heen in their book, *Thanks for the Feedback: The Science and Art of Receiving Feedback Well.*[1] We can't control another person or their words, but we can control our own actions and reactions.

In most instances, the best initial response is to take a deep breath and a step back. Let your first emotions subside, then prayerfully consider these three factors:

1. THE SOURCE

Who uttered the criticism, and what is their relationship to you? Was it a stranger? A distant acquaintance? A supervisor?

WOMEN SPEAK: CHALLENGES

What has been the most challenging for you as you have sought to obey God's calling?

- "Deciphering between God's calling and my own ambition. Am I trusting God with outcomes, or am I trying to manipulate outcomes?"—*Jenni*

- "My calling involves walking into deep waters with hurting people. Working with the heartbroken sometimes means your heart breaks from what you have to see."—*Chara*

- "Being tethered to my husband's job."—*Marlena*

- "Not being given the same amount of respect by other clergy."—*Val*

- "Believing in my gifts as much as God does and seeing myself through God's eyes."—*Jennifer*

- "Dealing with my parents and their expectations."—*Juliet*

- "The greatest challenge has been the effect ministry has on my family. Ministry is not a nine-to-five job, and I was spending more time with other peoples' kids than my own. I've no doubt my schedule contributed to the demise of my marriage."—*Allison*

- "Obeying without knowing."—*Jes*

A colleague? A close friend? What might be their motivation? Was it intended to be helpful or to tear down? As best you can, try to understand the person's feelings and perspective. (The best way to do this is to actually ask, if possible, rather than ascribe motive.)

2. THE TRUTH

What was said? No, really: what was *actually* communicated? Note that this is different from what you *heard* or *felt*—although you need to be honest about those, as well. Stone and Heen note that criticism can set off emotional responses based on one of three triggers: Truth Triggers (the content of the criticism), Relationship Triggers (the relationship between giver and receiver), and Identity Triggers (how it makes us feel about ourselves).[2] Take some time to identify what triggers might be at play in your situation, and recognize the human tendency to downplay our weaknesses and overemphasize our strengths.

Next, do your best—perhaps with the help of an objective third party—to identify reality in relationship to these triggers. Is there any truth to the criticism? What is the reality of your relationship with the criticizer? And most importantly, what is the reality of your identity as a child of God and your calling as a follower of Christ? American pastor and author Raymond Edman exhorted, "Never doubt in the dark what God told you in the light." As king Mufasa told his young son, Simba, "Remember who you are." And remember that your life and leadership are to be lived not for the masses but before a true audience of one.

3. YOUR RESPONSE

Once you have reflected on the source and the truth of a particular criticism, you can determine the appropriate response. Perhaps the words stung but they were uttered by a faithful friend (Proverbs 27:6). If so, the proper response might be to thank that person. Maybe the criticism was blatantly untrue, and you need to decide whether to ignore or confront it. Perhaps you realize there are larger dynamics at play, such as organizational power structures or perceived personal threats. In those types of situations, you must consider when, where, and how to wisely communicate truth and love. Or perhaps you recognize that your initial reaction was rooted in your own fears and insecurities, and that you need to work on your own emotional and spiritual health.

By focusing on our relationship with God and our own reactions, we can take much of the negative power—if not the initial sting—out of criticism.

Doubt

Doubt—defined as lack of confidence—sometimes develops in response to external criticism, but it can also spring up from within. It is not unusual for women leaders to experience feelings of uncertainty, insignificance, and lack of qualification regarding their ministry. After all, Satan will do anything he can to thwart anyone on mission for Christ.

As with criticism, the bigger concern is not whether we will have doubts, but what we will do with them. There are two possible responses: fear or faith. We can shrink back in fear, letting doubt keep us from obeying God's calling.

But with the Lord as the stronghold of our lives, we have nothing—and no one—to fear (Psalm 27:1).

The other option is to proceed in faith, which *does not require certainty.* In fact, certainty can be a hindrance to faith. As Hebrews 11:1 reminds us, faith *is* assurance about what we do not see. The opposite of doubt is not certainty but courage. And our courage is fortified by clinging closely to Christ. "Unsure of ourselves, we are sure of God," reminds Os Guinness.[3] Listen for God's voice over the myriad of others that clamor for our attention. Stay rooted in the one who has overcome the world and whose strength is made perfect in our weakness.

"My ability to reach my potential is limited by my self-doubt and fear," acknowledged Jennifer, an alcohol-and-addictions counselor and licensed minister. "I have a big passion, big desire, and big dream that I play over and over again in my mind's eye. It's all put together, launched, successful, and most of all, for him.

"Yet, yet . . . the Accuser attempts to remind me of who I was and that I will not measure up by God's standards," she continued. "But then the Holy Spirit reminds me that I am his standard, his masterpiece, created in his image. I am able to do all things through Christ who strengthens me. I am there, sitting on my bike, putting my helmet on, ready to ride this out. I just need to hit the throttle."

Waiting and Not Hearing

Sometimes, doubts rise to the surface because it seems that God has fallen silent. You ask God for clear direction. You're eager to take next steps, or maybe you're desperate for a word of reassurance. You strain to hear his voice. But: nothing. You keep asking, waiting, listening—a few more days, weeks, months, perhaps even years or decades. As Beth Booram writes, "The ache of want we want is so strong and insistent we can begin to feel desperate for its fulfillment."[4]

Since the day I heard God's call at the sports desk, I had faithfully served him in some type of youth ministry. One night almost fifteen years later, I stood on the concourse of a packed sports arena, taking in the energy of thousands of teens lifting their voices in worship at a major youth conference. Suddenly, the music and lights seemed to fade out, and in that pulsing arena I once again heard that still, small, yet infinitely clear voice: *This isn't you anymore.*

"What?" my spirit replied.

This isn't you anymore, the voice repeated. *You've faithfully served in youth ministry for many years. But I am calling you out of youth ministry and into something new.*

Because I immediately recognized the voice of the Lord, I felt no anxiety about this instruction. I simply responded, "Okay, great. What's next?"

And then the voice was gone. It would be years before I received a clear answer; years during which I begged God to show me what was next, to please answer my simple, earnest question. I began to doubt his goodness and faithfulness, my ability to hear his voice, and whether I would ever receive another clear calling. (And my season in this "waitland" lasted only three years. I have no idea how Moses hung in there for forty.)

If we experience what feels like divine silence, there are two truths to which we must cling.

First, *God's ways are higher than our ways.* "For my thoughts are not your thoughts, neither are your ways my ways," the Lord declares in Isaiah 55:8. Peter reminds us, "With the Lord a day is like a thousand years, and a thousand years are like a day" (2 Peter 3:8). God reminded Job that no human will ever fully comprehend the one who laid the foundations of the earth (Job 38–39). And Paul confirms rhetorically, "Who has known the mind of the Lord?" (1 Corinthians 2:16).

In other words, perceived silence does not mean that God is absent or not working. God is always at work behind the scenes, preparing the way for what he has next for you. Perhaps your next assignment is not ready or doesn't even exist at the moment.

Or perhaps *you* are not ready. Which brings us to the second truth: *God is more interested in our growth than our gifts.* "The process of being reoriented is as important as the planned outcome," writes Ken Costa. "Our cry is, 'How long?' but God's cry is, 'You can trust me.'"[5] While we ask how we can serve him, God says, "I want *you.*"

Several years ago, my husband practiced an extended fast. As part of this spiritual and physical discipline, he went on a prayer walk any time he felt hungry. (Yes, he walked and prayed a lot.) During one of these walks, he prayed for God to speak to him. He listened expectantly, but as he rounded the final bend and approached our driveway, he still had not heard anything. Just as he felt himself getting a bit annoyed, God broke into his thoughts with what felt like a winking reminder: *David, it's good that you are listening, but that doesn't obligate me to speak.* Point taken.

God does not fit himself into our schedules. The proper response to silence is faithfulness: to God, to what we already know to be true, and to our daily responsibilities and disciplines as we wait and trust in *his* faithfulness. He is present, he is at work, and "he will never leave you nor forsake you" (Deuteronomy 31:6), even when it seems that he is silent.

Dry Desert Place

Sometimes the challenge is not that God's voice seems absent but that our soul is parched. One leader referred to this as the "dry desert place," and leaders find themselves in this challenge just as much as anyone else. In his excellent book *Spiritual Rhythm: Being with Jesus Every Season of Your Soul,* Mark Buchanan describes this as a season of winter.[6] It may be brought on by external loss, such as death, a broken relationship, or a move. It may result from pushing ourselves too hard, too far, for too long. It may derive from a combination of factors.

Whatever the reason, the result is the same. This dry season is characterized by feelings of absence, abandonment, and aloneness in relationship to God and to others. When our spiritual or emotional vitality is low, it is difficult to hear God, to sense his presence, and to imagine—or even remember—seasons of vibrance and fruit.

Our grief is compounded by guilt. "The assumption many of us labor beneath is this: God can't be in winter. God has abandoned me, or I have wandered from him, but this bleakness—this fruitlessness—can't be blessed by him. If I loved God, if God loved me, I wouldn't be here," Buchanan writes.[7] He suggests that this season can be a tremendous gift, however: "Most of us have had our deepest encounters with Christ not on mountaintops but in valley floors."[8]

There is important work to be done in a dry season, but that work is not measured by external productivity. Rather, the chief task is prayer, even when—*especially* when—it feels laborious and fruitless. Depending on how depleted you are, it can take a while to begin to experience rehydration. We echo the Sons of Korah: "LORD, you are the God who saves me; day and night I cry out to you. May my prayer come before you; turn your ear to my cry" (Psalm 88:1-2). Again, this is an exercise in faith: in trusting that God is a loving Shepherd who will lead us beside quiet waters and refresh our souls (Psalm 23:2-3).

The secondary task during this season, Buchanan suggests, is pruning: to take stock of what may have brought you to this place, and to clip any of the tendencies that may have contributed to our dehydration. "Cut to nothing all that which gives nothing," Buchanan exhorts.[9] This is not to say that every dry season is the result of personal deficit. But I know all too well that we women leaders often feel so responsible for everyone else that we neglect our own well-being. It is only through intentional and sometimes intense prayer and pruning that we give God the space to refill the well that waters our ministry.

Hardship

Hardship refers to serious or ongoing difficulty, misfortune, or adversity; and like most of the other challenges we've already explored, it's pretty much guaranteed at some point as we follow our calling. "All journeys have a cost," Jennie

Allen maintains. "The path to our purpose here is rarely built comfortably."[10]

Sometimes the cost is asked by God, although "within the boundaries of loving God and loving others, the payment will be different for each of us."[11] Some may be asked to live and serve in obscurity, while others may have to pay the price of living and leading under the glare of a spotlight. Some may be called to an itinerant life, never staying in one place for long, while others may need to sacrifice by staying in one location, putting down roots, and denying their wanderlust. Some may be asked to give up material comfort and financial security, while others may be asked to bear the burden of responsibility for stewarding wealth.

Of hardships imposed by the fact of a fallen world, the list of possibilities is endless: physical or emotional health issues, ongoing relational conflicts, abuses of power, organizational dysfunction, institutional prejudice, natural disasters, even the threat of death. Sometimes the hardship is self-imposed, as we fight God for control of our lives.

Sarah, a forty-three-year-old regional director for an international-missions organization, has experienced all of the above during the course of her ministry. In her first three years on the mission field as a young married woman, Sarah experienced natural disasters, political unrest, terrorist threats, ministry-team issues, and health concerns, including a tropical disease that triggered bipolar disorder in her husband.

Sarah had felt God's call to be a missionary since she was ten years old. She met and married a man with a similar call to missions work in Southeast Asia. The couple thought they would serve there for many years. Instead, Sarah, her husband, and their eleven-month-old son had to be medically evacuated. "I was suddenly without a home, ministry, or job, and my life partner was mentally unstable," she recalled.

Sarah and her husband decided to move to Sydney, Australia, where they could help mobilize churches and individuals for their missions organization. The hardship continued, however. She and her husband struggled to navigate necessary changes to their roles at home and in ministry due to his ongoing health issues. Then another one of their children went through a season of crisis. The challenges of her ministry role pushed Sarah into her own emotional stress and eventual burnout.

Fifteen years after leaving for what she thought would be a lifetime calling to Southeast Asia, Sarah reflected on her journey, her doubts, and God's faithfulness: "As we were leaving the mission field, I wanted to question God and be angry, but we had hundreds, possibly thousands of people praying for us worldwide through our mission network. Complete strangers wrote to us, and we found that every need was miraculously met. I couldn't deny God's care and protection when doctors were suddenly where we needed them to be, visas were granted faster than normal, and personal relationships smoothed the way to make things easier."

Sarah also grappled with changes to her paradigm about marriage and ministry: "I entered marriage thinking that I would live life together in ministry with my husband. When he had to step back, I was devastated because I held tightly to the dream of doing ministry together."

Sarah sees now that God has used every part of her journey to prepare her for her current role with her mission agency, overseeing a significant portion of the organization's work in Australia. "Those experiences have prepared me to support others in their difficult times," she acknowledged.

Sarah also denies any notion that she is an exceptionally strong person. "The truth is that I have always battled low self-esteem and struggled with all the disappointments of not doing what I want to do," she said. "Calling, suffering, and submission are all mixed up together for me, but somehow result in joy. Only God can bring joy and victory in all of our mess.

"No matter what we suffer, God is still God," she concluded. "When everything falls apart, I start with that fact. We all need a strong conviction that we are in the place where God wants us; otherwise, we will throw in the towel as soon as we face difficulties or spiritual warfare." Sarah's story shows us two essential tasks we must undertake when responding to hardship: *reframing* and *reflecting*.

REFRAMING

During times of hardship, it's natural to focus on what is happening to us at the moment. But as servants of Christ, we need to remember a greater perspective. "Consider it pure joy, my brothers and sisters, whenever you face trials of many kinds, because you know that the testing of your faith produces perseverance," James writes (James 1:2-3). Paul points out, "We know that suffering produces perseverance; perseverance, character; and character, hope" (Romans 5:3-4). And Peter reminds us that those who follow Christ have a "living hope" and an eternal reward that should cause us to rejoice, even in seasons of grief and trials (1 Peter 1:3-7).

In other words, hardship is a gift. Sometimes hardship is

a severe mercy, but it is a demonstration of God's love none-theless. Only this perspective can give us gratitude and joy in the face of hardship. Whatever the cause of our suffering, God can use it to shape us more to his likeness. Even if this is the only redeeming earthly value we gain from a difficult experience, God's Word tells us that this is enough:

> I consider everything a loss because of the surpassing worth of knowing Christ Jesus my Lord, for whose sake I have lost all things. I consider them garbage, that I may gain Christ and be found in him, not having a righteousness of my own that comes from the law, but that which is through faith in Christ— the righteousness that comes from God on the basis of faith. I want to know Christ—yes, to know the power of his resurrection and participation in his sufferings, becoming like him in his death.
>
> PHILIPPIANS 3:8-10

At age forty-nine, Lindy was diagnosed with breast can-cer. As with many who experience this hardship, her world was turned upside down overnight. Her fruitful ministry for a Christian arts organization was put on hold as she entered treatment and began to imagine and grieve losses such as not seeing her sons graduate high school and college, get married, or have children. Yet in the midst of the grief, Lindy has been a shining light of hope and joy. In fact, Lindy believes her cancer is a part of her God-given calling.

"I believe our only purpose as humans walking this earth is to bring glory to God through how we live our lives," she said. "And sometimes, hard or difficult circumstances draw people into our story much quicker than easy situations.

"I have friends who are now able to open up a conversation about God with their neighbor," Lindy reported. "Praise God! And then there are some in my life who have also been selected to endure the cancer journey and they aren't so fond of the journey. I am also able to help them, by example, grasp this special opportunity to give God the glory despite their circumstance. And the testimonies and stories my boys and husband will have (and do have) . . . oh my goodness.

"I now see every day as a gift instead of an obligation," Lindy continued. "I am truly grateful for the opportunity to be here for another day, week, month, and year. I love my life and would never, *ever* go back to my pre-cancer days. I have been changed for the good, and I believe the quality of life for those around me has improved, as well." Lindy's absolute joy and faith on this most difficult path is a continual source of inspiration (and amazement) to me.

REFLECTING

In the midst of difficult seasons, it is important to spend time reflecting on the nature and lessons of our hardship in order to learn and grow for the future. For example, is the hardship the result of factors out of our control, or the natural consequence of our own choices? Our prayerful reflection will help us with the work of reframing and will also help us discern the best response. What changes do you need to make to better tend to your mental, emotional, and spiritual health? What do you need to take responsibility for, repent of, or forgive?

RECONCILING THE PAST

According to Mark Buchanan in *Spiritual Rhythm*, there are two unhealthy paths we can take as we reflect on past challenges: unforgiveness or nostalgia. Unforgiveness may seem the more dangerous of the two, but Buchanan believes they are opposite sides of the same coin:

> Nostalgia paints history gold, just as unforgiveness paints it black. . . . Both unforgiveness and nostalgia share the trait of an unreconciled past. Nostalgia is a vain attempt to reconcile the past through wistfulness, whereas unforgiveness is a doomed attempt to reconcile it through vengeance. The past is actually only ever reconciled through four things: thankfulness, forgiveness, acceptance, and repentance.[12]

Set aside some time to reflect on and reconcile a challenge from your past. Describe the situation, then list the four actions: thankfulness, forgiveness, acceptance, and repentance. Ask yourself the following questions:

1. **Thankfulness.** What can I be thankful for from this situation? What good has come from it?
2. **Forgiveness.** Who must I still forgive?
3. **Acceptance.** What do I need to just accept in order to move on?
4. **Repentance.** To whom [or Whom] must I repent, and for what?

In addition, during trying times, it is normal to question God's direction. Is a particular hardship roadblock telling us to turn around or a challenge to overcome? The answer could be different for every person and for each situation, and it may not be clear until months or years down the road. Hardship is not an automatic sign that you are either on the right path or on the wrong one. Be cautious, therefore, to not immediately ascribe a particular spiritual meaning to your (or anyone else's) difficulty. Maybe God has placed you in a difficult situation to *bring* the change. And maybe his primary purpose is to refine your character.

About two years after we left North Carolina, I stood in the doorway between our bedroom and bathroom, toothbrush in hand, and reflected with Dave about the difficulty of that season. "Why was it so hard?" I asked him, only somewhat rhetorically. I felt it wasn't for lack of effort on our part. And yet, although we experienced some fruitfulness, the majority of our time there felt like an uphill trudge, professionally and relationally—certainly more challenging than anything we had experienced to that point.

"I don't know, but I'm glad we are here now," he responded. I had to agree. We had experienced so much healing, both individually and in our marriage. Our boys were thriving. Our ministry was bearing fruit. We were in a really good place.

Yet my question went unanswered. I let the conversation drop.

Two weeks later, I was driving in my car, listening to music, minding my own business and not even consciously thinking of my question, when *that voice* interrupted my thoughts once again.

You weren't ready.

I snapped to attention. What?

Remember that question you asked a few weeks ago? the voice continued. I knew immediately.

You weren't ready, he repeated gently. *You had to go through that hard season, and I had to work on some rough edges in your life before you would be ready to handle the abundance you are experiencing now.*

His words were piercing—and absolutely correct. I felt my entire body release in complete peace. He knew best. Of course he did. I would never want to go through that hard season again, but I wouldn't trade it for the world because of what God did through it.

"Thank you," I whispered.

Brokenness

Sometimes the hardship crushes us. Whether it's by opposition, crisis, loss, long-lived difficulty that eventually sucks the life out of us, or our own actions, we may find ourselves completely broken. The tears seem endless, our hope nearly snuffed. The words of others bring little comfort. At that moment, death itself may seem a preferred alternative.

The psalmist David sums up the experience in what is perhaps the most depressing worship song ever written:

> Have mercy on me, LORD, for I am faint;
> heal me, LORD, for my bones are in agony.
> My soul is in deep anguish.
> How long, LORD, how long?

Turn, LORD, and deliver me;
    save me because of your unfailing love.
Among the dead no one proclaims your name.
    Who praises you from the grave?

I am worn out from my groaning.

All night long I flood my bed with weeping
    and drench my couch with tears.
My eyes grow weak with sorrow;
    they fail because of all my foes.

PSALM 6:2-7

I can tell you from experience: it's a horrible, awful feeling. And yet, whether we can "feel" him or not, God is there.

If you feel crushed, if you are mourning, if you can't see the dawn for the present darkness, the Bible promises God's presence and special care to you.

- The Lord is near to the brokenhearted (Psalm 34:18).
- The Good Shepherd refreshes our souls and comforts us (Psalm 23:3-4).
- God does not despise a broken and contrite spirit (Psalm 51:17).
- The Lord longs to be gracious to us and will rise up to show us compassion (Isaiah 30:18).
- He revives the spirit of the lonely and contrite (Isaiah 57:15).
- God heals the brokenhearted and binds their wounds (Psalm 147:3).

- His unfailing love is priceless (Psalm 36:7).
- Those who mourn will be comforted (Matthew 5:4).
- The Father of compassion comforts us in all our troubles (2 Corinthians 1:3-4).
- The God of all grace restores us and makes us strong, firm, and steadfast (1 Peter 5:10).

In addition, brokenness does not automatically disqualify you for ministry or leadership. It may mean you need to take some time away to heal, but God can redeem all brokenness for his glory.

Nicole was forty-two years old and enjoying a fulfilling and significant leadership role at a large church when her world fell apart. As she sat in her brokenness, Nicole felt she had lost everything. She wondered if she would ever experience healing in her heart, forgiveness in relationships, or restoration to ministry.

But as she continued to make the difficult, daily choice to stay with her pain and the situation, Nicole experienced reassurances not only of God's deep love for her but also of her calling to ministry—not despite her brokenness but because of it.

"The first week after everything fell apart, I knew more than ever that God had not removed his calling; he had confirmed it," she said. "God said, 'I have plans for you. And these plans include telling people who don't know how much I love them.'

"I've been a Christian most of my life, but I didn't really believe that God loved me until I was faced with my own failure in such a dramatic way," Nicole continued. "In the midst of the humiliation and failure and shame and all that went with it, there was a peace that existed in my heart that wasn't there before. I had a compassion for people who have never once heard, 'God loves you, and God's grace is bigger than this.'

"I hate that it took this for me to get that, but in a sense, I'm so grateful now because I don't have any doubts that God loves me. I don't have any doubts that he can use even me," Nicole reflected. "How I wish I could take back the pain I've caused. But God told me, 'What happened isn't okay, but I'm going to use it for my purposes.' God isn't confined by my failure. He can use it for his glory and our good."

One word of caution: While brokenness may not disqualify you from future ministry or leadership and can even become a source of greater strength and compassion, it is *imperative* that you take the time needed to reflect, rest, and recover before resuming ministry. That may be weeks, months, or even years. *Do not rush this process.* We can inflict tremendous harm on others if we attempt to minister out of our own unaddressed wounds. Seek accountability, support, and professional help to regain stability and strength before going back into the field.

CHALLENGES AND CHANGING COURSE

When we experience challenges, it is perfectly normal to question our calling, or at least to consider whether it is time to make a change from our current ministry. In fact, I would argue that these questions are an important and healthy part of an ongoing conversation with God about our calling.

We should not let challenges cripple us with doubt, but we should always remain open to the possibility that God is using a challenge to redirect our steps.

As we pause to listen to God's direction, we might hear one of three instructions:

1. Stay the course.
2. Stop and wait for further instruction.
3. Change course.

Unless you have sensed clear direction that your calling has been paused or will be changed, the default response should generally be to stay the course. You may need to make adjustments as you respond, but challenges should not automatically be viewed as roadblocks or closed doors.

There are times when God may tell you to stop, however. Sometimes, the break is just a short pause to catch your breath; other times, God may be instructing you to be still for a longer season. You may want to press on, but it is important to wait on God's direction and trust his timing.

The third possibility is that God may direct you to a change of course or calling. Although your primary call to follow Christ never changes, your secondary calling can change. Sometimes it is broadened; other times, it changes entirely. These changes may result from life stage, the realitics of a particular situation, or from what Gordon MacDonald calls a "fresh call" from God.[13] And, as with my calling out of youth ministry, there may be a long pause between the "stop" and the next "go." God may call you *away* from something before he calls you *to* something else.

WOMEN SPEAK: HAS YOUR CALLING CHANGED?

Has your calling changed over the course of your life?

- "I think my calling has expanded and contracted over the years. The early years of coming alongside my husband in ministry with lots of energy, then years of raising a family and bringing teens into our home, turned into our teenagers bringing their friends into our life, as well. Empty nesting feels different. My influence and opportunities have changed, as well. I believe I'm still drawn to hospitality, but it has had many faces."—*Joyce*

- "I'd say there are parts that have fallen away. I used to do a lot more administration, but it turned out that was less related to my calling—I just had a certain ability to organize."—*Cassia*

- "I would say it's been added to. God has continued to use my past and present experiences to enhance and build my heart."—*Sarah*

- "I believe my called vocation was ministry, particularly to the church, but I was stopped by people in power from living that out. My vocation is now being lived out as a chaplain in a 250-bed hospital-and-trauma center."—*Nancy*

- "I used to think my calling was just to be available to anybody and everybody, which really turned out badly. I have been through a ten-year process of trauma recovery and had to necessarily pull back from a lot of stuff. In the past year, I've felt like God is calling me to something, but I'm honestly still not positive what."—*Jes*

During these times of waiting or redirection, we may discover that our calling and our identity have become intertwined. It can be difficult to separate what we "do" from who we "are," especially if we have been doing a particular work for a long time. As a result, a change in calling may also challenge our sense of self-worth.

Imagine for a moment that God asked you to let go of your current calling. What is your gut response? Do you tense up at the possibility, or do you feel a sense of peace and release? Obeying our calling should be fulfilling. But our calling should not be our primary identity.

"*Who* I am, before *why* I am," reminds Ken Costa. "So often we try to skip the first to end up with the second."[14]

When we equate our calling with our identity, challenges such as criticism are magnified because it feels like the critic is challenging *us*, not just our work. In addition, the likelihood of burnout, spiritual dryness, and emotional codependence increases exponentially.

"As soon as a leader's identity gets bound up in their title, their clout, their hero status, their power, or their position, they will serve that position like a slave, until they ultimately burn out," asserts Sharon Hodde Miller. "And perhaps even worse, they will trample and manipulate others in order to maintain it. . . .When our identities are bound up in our work, then our service is anything but selfless. Instead, we are putting ourselves first."[15]

The antidote is threefold: First, maintain a posture of constant watch regarding the source of your identity. Second, enlist others to hold you accountable and to keep you grounded. Third, stay close to Christ, seeking to imitate his servant mind-set (Philippians 2:1-9).

WHAT NOW?

No matter what your particular challenge may be as you pursue your calling as a leader, there are several general truths to remember.

First, *following your calling* will *involve challenges.* Those challenges will look different for every person. Some may be preventable, but most are not. The first step toward accepting challenges is expecting them.

A second and related point is this: *Challenges or the lack of them—are not automatically a measure of a Christ follower's spiritual maturity, faith, or obedience.* As Jesus reminds us in Matthew 5:45, "[The Father] causes his sun to rise on the evil and the good, and sends rain on the righteous and the unrighteous." Also, while challenges *may* serve to redirect our calling, be cautious of immediately interpreting challenges as open or closed doors.

Third, God wants *you.* More than anything that you can *do* in service to him, God wants to shape your *being.* He values the condition of your heart over the works of your hands. Challenges are a means for discipleship—the crucible in which you might be formed more closely into the image of Christ. Challenges also help us loosen our grip on idols, including those related to our identity.

Fourth, in light of the first three truths, and in response to any challenge: *Cling closely to Christ.* Whether your challenge is criticism, waiting for God to speak, spiritual dryness, hardship, or utter brokenness—fix your eyes on Jesus, the "pioneer and perfecter" of our faith (Hebrews 12:2). Meditate on his love, his goodness, his suffering, his sacrifice, his forgiveness, his faithfulness. Trust his work and his timing (Romans 8:28). Only in Christ's power and presence can we stay the course of our calling in the face of challenges.

CONTINUE THE CONVERSATION

» What challenges are you currently experiencing as you seek to follow your calling? Which of these are external, and which are internal?

» When was a time that you experienced God's faithfulness in the midst of a challenge?

» What challenges from your past do you need to reconcile in order to avoid either nostalgia or unforgiveness?

» Do you have a healthy distinction between your ministry calling and your identity?

BENEDICTION

We have come together on this journey of finding and following our calling as women ministry leaders. We have looked at God's Word, we have listened to others' stories, we have explored challenging issues, we have asked ourselves hard questions.

A leader's calling can be weighty, confusing, empowering, life-giving, hope-filled. As women of influence, we discern and step into our calling with a heavier burden of responsibility because how we live out our calling impacts every person we lead and serve. But we are not alone on this journey of finding and following our calling. God is the one who has called us, and he is leading us forward. And many sisters walk beside us, sharing stories of their journey, offering hope and perspective and whispering encouragement, as they've done throughout this book.

As we step out on the unique pathways that God has created for each one of us, let us together receive this benediction.

To those straining and struggling to hear your calling:
May the whispers of the Spirit grow ever louder and clearer until they fill your heart in an unmistakeable crescendo.

To those facing internal doubts about your worthiness to do what God is asking you to do:
May you know and gain strength from your Father's utter delight in you and in who he has created you to be.

To those facing external limitations to exercising your call:
May you respond with grace, peace, and patience toward humans while remaining obedient to the clear voice of the Lord.

To those currently going it alone:
May you know the warm embrace and empowering strength of the community of God's gathered people.

To those wanting to do more in this season of life:
May God grant you patience as you wait, trusting in the knowledge that his timing is perfect.

And to those needing to do less:
May God loosen your grip and take your hands in his, and may you grow content to simply be *instead of anxious to constantly* do.

To those working out their calling in the context of marriage:
May your marriage be your strongest ministry, the embodiment of God's grace and love and a source of strength and joy to all, including yourself.

To those whose souls are parched:
May God provide streams of living water to refresh, replenish, and restore dry soil to fertile ground.

For those who have crashed, burned, lost, or failed:
May God lift your head, remind you every day of his tender mercies, and replace your tears of sorrow with twirling steps of joy.

To those facing financial limitation and strain:
May you experience hope in the promise of provision by the God who owns the cattle on a thousand hills.

To those enjoying a season of abundance:
May you feast with delight and share generously with others in gratitude to the Lord of the harvest.

To those who have walked ahead on this journey:
May God bless you for clearing the way for those of us behind you on the path. Let us learn from your example and pave the way for those who come after us.

And to those who are just starting out:
May God fan the flames of your passion and may your energy and enthusiasm burn long and bright, inspiring all those around you.

My dear sisters, "stand firm. Let nothing move you. Always give yourselves fully to the work of the Lord, because you know that your labor in the Lord is not in vain" (1 Corinthians 15:58).

Take courage, and be encouraged. You are unique, and you are not alone.

You go nowhere by accident.
Wherever you go, God is sending you.

Wherever you are, God has put you there; He has a purpose in you being there.
Christ, who indwells you, has something He wants to do through you where you are.
Believe this and go in His grace and love and power.
Amen.

RICHARD HALVORSON[1]

TESTIMONY

Throughout this book, you have read about the dozens of women I was privileged to interview for this project. After listening to their unique stories, I concluded many conversations with the question, "What have you learned about God and about calling as you have walked the path set before you?" Their responses, collected below, testify powerfully to God's nature, character, and work in their lives. May their words encourage, challenge, and strengthen you on your journey.

- "If God is for me in this, nothing can be against me in it. I just have to keep going."

- "As I bumble along this path, I've learned that God is nothing but good."

- "Just listen to what God is telling you and try not to discount it. Just stop and listen and try to consider what God might be laying on your heart."

- "Calling can come in so many different forms."

- "I can really trust him. He's not setting me up for failure."

- "Calling is a restless desire that may morph depending on life circumstances, but the called one will seek to find a way to fulfill the calling in all circumstances."

- "Usually, God's leading is not toward comfort. It is toward discomfort, vulnerability, exposing our weaknesses, because that's usually where healing comes."

- "No one becomes needed or important enough to be exempt from demonstrating the patience, love, and mercy of Jesus."

- "God is my breath when I can't breathe. He calms the storms in my mind and gives me ears to listen to people's heart. God's willingness to teach this old dog new tricks amazes me, and I am so very thankful to be used by him."

- "Hold everything a lot more loosely."

- "He's definitely more patient than I thought he was. Also, God is not 'using' me. He is living with me. He is inviting me into what he's doing."

- "God is always bigger than my ideas of how things should work."

- "God teaches and reaches each of us in different ways."

- "It matters that I obey."

- "You cannot deny your calling. You may disobey it, but it doesn't go away. If you pretend it's not there, God doesn't change his mind."

- "I've learned that God really does desire my greatest good."

- "I have learned the sound of his voice, the presence of the Holy Spirit. I can choose to accept the invitation or not. But I've learned that if I say no, he'll take the idea to someone else. It is always in my best interests—and the most interesting—when I choose to say yes to those quiet nudgings."

- "Faith is foolish. It's not practical. It's not necessarily responsible in the way society says responsibility should work."

- "It sounds trite, but what I've really learned is that he is good. And that his ways, even though they may not seem right, are good. They're right. I don't have to control it any more."

- "Calling is not static. Be open to it, because what starts out as clearly a position of calling for you in one year could take you somewhere else and be just as anointed and appointed as where you were a year ago."

- "God can do what he wants. I've seen in my life that it's not a 'you need to fix this now' kind of thing. It's a very gradual and encouraging push for more intimacy with him and more trust in him."

- "God is so full of surprises. I tend to get irritated by surprises. I almost have found myself with an attitude of, 'God, how dare you!,' which is ludicrous because God is the one who made me!"

- "That my being has purpose, that I am capable to do and be who God has made me to be, and that it's okay for the path to evolve."

- "I've learned to move with God. When he moves, I move. He takes one step, I take one step. He waits, I wait. When I do that, it's so much better. There is a peace and a fulfillment during that time."

- "God has perfect timing, never moving too soon or too late."

- "Our desire and God's desire aren't so distinct as what I used to think."

- "I am so overwhelmed with God's faithfulness and his goodness in it. Even in the darkest moments, he's there."

- "I don't have to be perfect; I just have to walk in perfect obedience—or frankly, just walk with some semblance of obedience. He graces me out when I eventually choose obedience."

- "For a very long time, I thought calling and job description were synonymous. But it's less about your job description and more about expressing your calling in every single aspect of your life. My job is going to shift, but I'll always be living into my calling."

- "When you hear the call, you just have to start taking steps toward it. You just have to start somewhere, and God will start making it more clear."

- "This past year, I feel like God keeps speaking the word *adventure* to me."

- "It's so important to listen to the Lord—just to be attentive, to really trust. Be pliable, moldable."

- "He is faithful . . . always. God can do far more than I can imagine."

- "Plans are great, but things are never going to go as planned. Trust the process and that God uses everything, even when it seems like I went in the wrong direction. I didn't necessarily go in the wrong direction; there was something that God had to teach me so that I could get on that path."

- "His idea is always better than mine. I have a pretty limited view of everything. Also, God is not in a hurry. I want to move the time line a little faster. If I wait, the slow simmer is better than the microwave."

- "God doesn't always call through institutions or in the ways that I want."

- "The more you say no to God, the more you purposefully turn your head away while he is trying to speak, the more you aren't going to hear him anymore. Not because he's not trying, but because you've hardened your heart to him."

- "God bestows a lot more grace than we put on ourselves."

- "I've learned how faithful God is. If he gives me an idea, he'll show me what to do with it. He will navigate the path, bring the people he wants me to meet, introduce me to teachers from whom I can learn, and make the connections that only he can make. If I dream too far ahead, I'm reminded that he's in this moment. *This one*. Always."

- "I've learned that he is so loving. And even when we are stupid with doubt, he is loving and merciful and he wants us to go along beside him and trust that he's got the way figured out."

- "There is always hope."

Now to him who is able to do immeasurably more than all we ask or imagine, according to his power that is at work within us, to him be glory in the church and in Christ Jesus throughout all generations, for ever and ever! Amen.

EPHESIANS 3:20-21

ACKNOWLEDGMENTS

The book you hold in your hands lists my name as sole author, but so many have contributed to make it a reality. Just saying "thank you" to these people seems woefully inadequate, but I trust that those mentioned below know me well enough to understand the deep sentiment behind my simple words.

Thank-you:

To Christ (of course), the Giver of all good things, my Savior, and my all in all.

To Dave, my biggest cheerleader, my soul mate, my perfect counterbalance, and my partner in life and ministry for twenty-five years and counting.

To Taylor and Jamison, my tall, strong, kind, talented, and hilarious sons, who keep me grounded and serve as daily reminders of God's great grace.

To Brewster, my sweet, adorable, and very spoiled beagle, who would snore in his dog bed near my desk until I was deep into my writing, at which point invariably he would rise, stretch, and systematically bring me every. single. toy. from his bin in an effort to entice me to play.

To my small group and church community at New Hope Church, who embody what it truly means to be the family of God. You have brought me hope, healing, and a whole lot of laughter.

To Brian and Joyce Farka and Rick and Teresa Dunn, who have been immeasurably influential on my life, faith, and ministry from my formative years. My love and gratitude for you are no secret. And to the countless other friends who have walked beside me during the course of my decades-long journey. I am humbled and blessed by such a great and loyal cloud of witnesses.

To Amy Jackson, who instigated the idea of this book and served as its original champion. To Rob Toal and Jake Walsh at *Christianity Today*, for encouraging me to dream bigger. And to Marshall Shelley, who first brought me into the *CT* family.

To Cherie Lowe, for her constant cheerleading, our mastermind meetings, and the Qdoba conversation that helped move this book from an idea to an outline.

To the members of the Women & Calling Book Team group on Facebook, for strengthening the book—and me—through your continued support, encouragement, and input.

To Keely Boeving and Greg Johnson at WordServe Literary Group, for the trust of their representation. And to Tricia Lott Williford, for making the introduction.

To the team at NavPress and Tyndale: What a joy to partner with such like-minded colaborers. To Don Pape, publisher extraordinaire, for his humble leadership and tireless encouragement. To Caitlyn Carlson, who stewarded this book from contract to completion and made me a better writer in the process. To Elizabeth Schroll, for her incredible copyediting eye. To Robin Bermel, for managing the myriad of publication and publicity details. And to Jennifer Ghionzoli for the beautiful cover design and Dean Renninger for the perfect painting.

Thanks for being my village. I love you all.

SPECIAL THANKS

To all the women who shared their experiences for this book: Oh, my goodness. What a privilege to hear, hold, and share your stories. I wish I had room in these pages to tell every part of every one of them. Thank you for your trust, your honesty, your vulnerability. Your stories have moved and inspired me deeply, and I know without a doubt that God will use them powerfully in the lives of many others, as well.

Carmille	Jana	Carolyn
Dorothy	Jes	Tammi
Emilie	Ashley	Janette
Sherry	Susan	Joyce
Marlena	Nicole	Jill
Juliet	Caroline	Jenni
Denise	Cherie	Ellen
Amy	Melanie	Laura
Pam	Kelly	Sarah
Nancy	Sharon	Allison
Lindy	Laura	Fran

Andrea	Jessica	Kate
Elizabeth	Cassia	Sydney
Kris	Amanda	Tricia
Ashley	Sarah	Kellie
LeeAnn	Val	Kara
Polly	Jennifer	Amanda
Jana	Chara	Jillian
Pauline	Stacey	Cynthia
Teresa	Cortney	Julie

Why Bother?

Because right now, there is   someone
out there with
a wound   in the exact shape
                                        of your words.

SEAN THOMAS DOUGHERTY, from *The Second O of Sorrow*

REFERENCES

Acuff, Jon. *Quitter: Closing the Gap Between Your Day Job and Your Dream Job.* Nashville: Harper Collins Religious, 2015.

Allender, Dan. *To Be Told: Know Your Story, Shape Your Future.* Colorado Springs: WaterBrook, 2005.

Barnett, Matthew. *The Cause within You: Finding the One Great Thing God Created You to Do in This World.* Carol Stream, IL: Tyndale, 2011.

Cloud, Henry. *Necessary Endings: The Employees, Businesses, and Relationships that All of Us Have to Give Up in Order to Move Forward.* New York: HarperCollins, 2010.

Crumley, Valetta Steel, and Edward Erny. *Another Valley, Another Victory, Another Love.* Greenwood: OMS International, 1997.

Dellenbaugh, Alison. "When Your Calling Feels too Small." *Women Leaders.* May 29, 2014. http://www.christianitytoday.com/women-leaders/2014 /may/when-your-calling-feels-too-small.html.

Desiring God. "Here We Stand: A 31-Day Journey with Heroes of the Reformation." Accessed March 20, 2018. https://www.desiringgod.org /here-we-stand.

Glass, Cassia. "Don't Quit Your Day Job." *Cassia's Place: Thoughts on Faith, Family, and Finding Purpose* (blog). March 22, 2017. https://cassiaglass .com/2017/03/22/dont-quit-your-day-job/.

Graves, Marlena. "My Difficult Past Makes Me a Better Leader." *Christianity Today.* November 2, 2015. http://www.christianitytoday.com/women -leaders/2015/november/my-difficult-past-makes-me-better-leader.html.

Johnson, Bill. *The Supernatural Power of a Transformed Mind: 40-Day Devotional and Personal Journal.* Shippensburg, PA: Destiny Image, 2011.

Leach, Tara Beth. *Emboldened: A Vision for Empowering Women in Ministry.* Downers Grove: InterVarsity Press, 2018.

Lobdell, Stephanie Dyrness. "My Winding Road to the Pastorate." *Christianity Today.* July 25, 2017. http://www.christianitytoday.com/women-leaders /2017/july/my-winding-road-to-pastorate.html.

Lowe, Cherie. *Slaying the Debt Dragon: How One Family Conquered Their Money Monster and Found an Inspired Happily Ever After.* Carol Stream, IL: Tyndale, 2015.

Lyons, Rebekah. *Freefall to Fly: A Breathtaking Journey Toward a Life of Meaning.* Nashville: LifeWay, 2014.

MacDonald, Gordon. *A Resilient Life: You Can Move Ahead No Matter What.* Nashville: Thomas Nelson, 2004.

MacFadyen, Heather. "Motherhood, Career, and Identity: Kat Armstrong." *God Centered Mom* (blog). June 26, 2017. http://godcenteredmom.com /2017/06/26/motherhood-career-identity-kat-armstrong-ep-171/.

Manglos, Jen. "My Burnout Led to a Breakthrough." *Christianity Today.* November 9, 2015. http://www.christianitytoday.com/women-leaders /2015/november/my-burnout-led-to-breakthrough.html.

Marsh, Karen Wright. "Take Delight in Your Passions." *Christianity Today.* November 2, 2017. https://www.christianitytoday.com/women-leaders /2017/november/take-delight-in-your-passions.html.

Mateer, Julia. "Discover Your God-Given Calling." *Christianity Today.* February 7, 2013. https://www.christianitytoday.com/women-leaders /2013/february/discover-your-god-given-calling.html.

Meredith, Cara. "Discomfort Clarified My Calling." *Christianity Today.* February 9, 2017. http://www.christianitytoday.com/women-leaders/2017 /february/discomfort-clarified-my-calling.html.

Miller, Sharon Hodde. "Women, Calling, and Guilt." *Christianity Today.* January 28, 2016. http://www.christianitytoday.com/women-leaders/2016 /january/women-calling-and-guilt.html.

Preaching Today. "A Benediction About Serving Wherever You Are." Accessed September 20, 2018. https://www.preachingtoday.com/illustrations/2016 /november/5112116.html.

Raynor, Jordan. "Three Questions for Discerning Your Calling." *Relevant Magazine.* May 29, 2019. https://relevantmagazine.com/article/3-questions -for-discerning-your-calling/.

Theology of Work. "The Call to Belong to Christ and Participate in His Redemptive Work in the World." Accessed March 20, 2018. https:// www.theologyofwork.org/key-topics/vocation-overview-article/types-of -gods-calling.

REFERENCES

Thomas, Tiffany. "Troublesome Women Preachers." *Christianity Today.* November 23, 2015. http://www.christianitytoday.com/women-leaders /2015/november/troublesome-women-preachers.html.

Verner, Leslie. "Why I Left the Cult of 'Calling' (and You Should, Too)." *Relevant Magazine.* December 14, 2018. https://relevantmagazine.com /god/left-cult-calling/.

Westfall, Cynthia Long. *Paul and Gender: Reclaiming the Apostle's Vision for Men and Women in Christ.* Grand Rapids, MI: Baker Academic, 2016.

Wilkinson, Bruce, David Kopp, and Heather Kopp. *The Dream Giver: Following Your God-Given Destiny.* Colorado Springs: Multnomah, 2003.

Willard, Dallas. *Hearing God: Developing a Conversational Relationship with God.* Downers Grove, IL: InterVarsity Press, 2012.

NOTES

INTRODUCTION

1. Halee Gray Scott, *Dare Mighty Things: Mapping the Challenges of Leadership for Christian Women* (Grand Rapids, MI: Zondervan, 2014), 74.

2. Jennie Allen, *Restless: Because You Were Made for More* (Nashville: W Publishing, 2013), 41.

3. Tish Harrison Warren, *Liturgy of the Ordinary: Sacred Practices in Everyday Life* (Downers Grove, IL: InterVarsity Press, 2016), 22.

4. Frederick Buechner, *Wishful Thinking: A Seeker's ABC* (London: Mowbray, 1994), 118–19.

CHAPTER 1: WHAT IS CALLING?

1. Blue Letter Bible, s.v. "qara'," accessed July 24, 2019, https://www.blue letterbible.org/lang/lexicon/lexicon.cfm?page=2&strongs=h7121&t=kjv #lexResults.

2. Os Guinness, *The Call: Finding and Fulfilling God's Purpose for Your Life* (Nashville: W Publishing, 2018), 5.

3. Richard Robert Osmer, *The Teaching Ministry of Congregations* (Louisville, KY: Westminster John Knox, 2005), 177.

4. As quoted in J. Oswald Sanders, *Every Life Is a Plan of God: Discovering His Will for Your Life* (Grand Rapids, MI: Discovery House, 1992), chap. 6.

5. *Oxford Living Dictionaries*, s.v. "calling (*n.*)," accessed May 23, 2019, https://en.oxforddictionaries.com/definition/calling.

6. Parker J. Palmer, *Let Your Life Speak: Listening for the Voice of Vocation* (Somerset, NJ: John Wiley & Sons, 2015), 25.

7. *Merriam-Webster*, s.v. "calling (*n.*)," accessed May 23, 2019, https://www.merriam-webster.com/dictionary/calling.

8. Halee Gray Scott, *Dare Mighty Things: Mapping the Challenges of Leadership for Christian Women* (Grand Rapids, MI: Zondervan, 2014), 74.

9. Guinness, *The Call*, 81–82.

10. Theology of Work, "Calling & Vocation: Overview," accessed March 20, 2018, https://www.theologyofwork.org/key-topics/vocation-overview-article.

11. Guinness, *The Call*, 61.

12. Guinness, *The Call*, 81.

13. I am indebted to Francis Chan for this idea, although I can't recall when or where I heard him say it.

14. Guinness, *The Call*, 81.

15. Henry T. Blackaby and Avery T. Willis, *On Mission with God: Living God's Purpose for His Glory* (Nashville, TN: B&H, 2002), 36.

16. Rick Warren, *The Purpose Driven Life: What on Earth Am I Here For?* (Grand Rapids, MI: Zondervan, 2002), front flyleaf.

17. Dan Balow, "The Best Selling Christian Books of All Time," The Steve Laube Agency, June 28, 2016, https://stevelaube.com/best-selling-christian-books-time/.

18. Guinness, *The Call*, 80. See also *Merriam-Webster*, s.v. "vocation (*n.*)," accessed July 24, 2019, https://www.merriam-webster.com/dictionary/vocation.

19. Palmer, *Let Your Life Speak*, 4.

20. Palmer, *Let Your Life Speak*, 10.

21. Jennie Allen, *Restless: Because You Were Made for More* (Nashville: W Publishing, 2013), 35. Emphasis in original.

22. Sanders, *Every Life Is a Plan of God*, chap. 2.

23. Tish Harrison Warren, *Liturgy of the Ordinary: Sacred Practices in Everyday Life* (Downers Grove, IL: InterVarsity Press, 2016), 34.

24. Tara Beth Leach, *Emboldened: A Vision for Empowering Women in Ministry* (Downers Grove, IL: InterVarsity Press, 2017), 65–67.

CHAPTER 2: DISCERNING A CALL

1. Barna, "Three Trends on Faith, Work and Calling," February 11, 2014, https://www.barna.com/research/three-trends-on-faith-work-and-calling/.

2. See also Genesis 28:10-15; 37:5-9; 46:1-4; 1 Kings 3:5-15; Isaiah 6:1-8; Ezekiel, Daniel, Zechariah, and Amos.

3. J. Robert Clinton, *The Making of a Leader: Recognizing the Lessons and Stages of Leadership Development*, 2nd ed. (Colorado Springs, CO: NavPress, 2015), 26–27.

4. Jennie Allen, *Restless: Because You Were Made for More* (Nashville: W Publishing, 2013), 122.

5. Claude Hickman, *Live Life on Purpose: God's Purpose. Your Life. One Journey* (Enumclaw, WA: WinePress, 2011), 36.

6. Elizabeth Liebert, *The Way of Discernment: Spiritual Practices for Decision Making* (Louisville, KY: Westminster John Knox, 2008), 8.

7. Ken Costa, *Know Your Why: Finding and Fulfilling Your Calling in Life* (Nashville: W Publishing, 2016), 64.

8. I believe I am indebted to Andy Stanley for this concept, although I don't recall where or when he said it.

9. Hickman, *Live Life on Purpose*, 26.

10. J. Oswald Sanders, *Every Life Is a Plan of God: Discovering His Will for Your Life* (Grand Rapids, MI: Discovery House, 1992), chap. 1.

11. Elisabeth Elliot, *A Slow and Certain Light: Thoughts on the Guidance of God* (Waco, TX: Word Books, 1977), 77–87.

12. Elliot, *A Slow and Certain Light*, 77–87.

13. This list is inspired by and partially taken from Elisabeth Elliot (see pp. 37ff), although I edited and added to her list.

14. Elliot, *A Slow and Certain Light*, 88.

15. Ben Campbell Johnson, *Hearing God's Call: Ways of Discernment for Laity and Clergy* (Grand Rapids, MI: Eerdmans, 2002), chap. 6.

16. Sanders, *Every Life Is a Plan of God*, chap. 2.

17. Os Guinness, *The Call: Finding and Fulfilling God's Purpose for Your Life* (Nashville: W Publishing, 2018), 79.

18. Carmille Akande, "Did I Hear God Right?: Just Because You Feel Like a Failure Doesn't Mean You Weren't Called by God," Women Leaders. com, November 21, 2016, http://www.christianitytoday.com/women -leaders/2016/november/did-i-hear-god-right.html.

19. Johnson, *Hearing God's Call*, 27.

20. Johnson, *Hearing God's Call*, 23.

21. Jon Bloom, "Your Emotions Are a Gauge, Not a Guide," Desiring God (ministry website), August 3, 2012, https://www.desiringgod.org/articles /your-emotions-are-a-gauge-not-a-guide.

22. *Circum* = "around" and *stance* = "to stand."

23. Sanders, *Every Life Is a Plan of God*, chap. 4.

24. Sanders, *Every Life Is a Plan of God*, chap. 2.

25. Sanders, *Every Life Is a Plan of God*, chap. 2.

26. Liebert, *The Way of Discernment*, 18.

27. Beth A. Booram, *Starting Something New: Spiritual Direction for Your God-Given Dream* (Downers Grove, IL: InterVarsity Press, 2015), 36.

28. Sanders, *Every Life Is a Plan of God*, chap. 2.

29. To read about this prayer, see Mark E. Thibodeaux, "Try the Daily Examen," accessed September 20, 2018, https://www.loyolapress.com/our-catholic -faith/ignatian spirituality/examen-and-ignatian-prayer/how-can-i-pray -try-the-daily-examen.

30. Johnson, *Hearing God's Call*, chap. 7.

31. Allen, *Restless*, 18.

32. Johnson, *Hearing God's Call*, chap. 4.

33. Tyler Blanski, *An Immovable Feast: How I Gave Up Spirituality for a Life of Religious Abundance* (San Francisco: Ignatius Press, 2018), 89.

34. Costa, *Know Your Why*, 5.

35. Guinness, *The Call*, 253.

CHAPTER 3: CALLING AND AUTHORITY

1. Christians for Biblical Equality (CBE) and the Council for Biblical Manhood and Womanhood (CBMW) both claim the "biblical" perspective on the roles of women in marriage and ministry, even though the two organizations come to polar opposite conclusions. For an example of the passion behind these perspectives, see this summary of the 2019 controversy surrounding popular Bible teacher and author, Beth Moore: https://religionnews.com/2019/06/05/beth-moores-ministry-reignites -debate-over-whether-women-can-preach/.

2. The earliest biblical manuscripts indicate that Junia was a woman; in later translations (from the 12th century), this name was changed to the masculine *Junias*. Most scholars today affirm that Junia was indeed a woman. Even if Junia was not an apostle, Paul clearly recognized her as "among the apostles" and as a leader in the early church, even if her role is unclear. See https://juniaproject.com/who-was-junia/ and https://carm .org/junia-apostle.

3. Jeffrey Kranz, "All the 'One Another' Commands in the NT [Infographic]," March 9, 2014, https://overviewbible.com/one-another-infographic/.

4. Jennie Allen, *Restless: Because You Were Made for More* (Nashville: W Publishing, 2013), 192–93.

5. Allen, *Restless*, 192.

6. "Andy Stanley | Catalyst Atlanta 2006," July 9, 2007, in Catalyst Leader, https://youtu.be/xoigF3COwbE.

7. Ligonier Ministries, "The External Call," accessed June 20, 2019, https://www.ligonier.org/learn/devotionals/external-call/.

8. Sarah Bessey, "Your Calling Isn't Just Between You and God. How Community Discernment Can Help Women Recognize Their Gifts," *Christianity Today*, April 12, 2016, http://www.christianitytoday.com /women/2016/april/your-calling-isnt-just-between-you-and-god.html.

9. Friends General Conference, "Some Guidelines for Clearness for a Leading or Ministry under the Care of a Meeting," April 10, 2005, https://www .fgcquaker.org/sites/default/files/attachments/Guidelines%20for%20 Clearness%20for%20a%20Leading%20or%20Ministry.pdf.

10. Barna, "Meet Those Who 'Love Jesus but Not the Church,'" March 30, 2017, https://www.barna.com/research/meet-love-jesus-not-church/.

11. Os Guinness, *The Call: Finding and Fulfilling God's Purpose for Your Life* (Nashville: W Publishing, 2018), 138.

12. Allen, *Restless*, 190.

13. Mother Saint Teresa and Brian Kolodiejchuk, *Come Be My Light: The Private Writings of the "Saint of Calcutta"* (New York: Doubleday, 2007), 92.

14. Teresa and Kolodiejchuk, *Come Be My Light*, 45.

15. Teresa and Kolodiejchuk, *Come Be My Light*, 105.

16. Concordia Publishing House. "Did Luther Really Say, 'Here I Stand'?" *The Word Endures* (blog), April 18, 2016, https://blog.cph.org/around -the-house/did-luther-really-say-here-i-stand/.

CHAPTER 4: CALLING AND MARRIAGE

1. Susan Ackerman, "Women in Ancient Israel and the Hebrew Bible," April 2016, http://religion.oxfordre.com/view/10.1093/acrefore/978019934037 8.001.0001/acrefore-9780199340378-e-45.

2. Bible Gateway, "Chapter 2. Alphabetical Exposition of Named Bible Women," accessed April 18, 2018, https://www.biblegateway.com /resources/all-women-bible/Chapter-2-Alphabetical.

3. In addition to the four passages already identified (Acts 18:3; Acts 18:18; Romans 16:3; and Acts 18:24-26), this list also includes 1 Corinthians 16:19 and 2 Timothy 4:19.

4. Andreas Kostenberger, *The Bible's Teaching on Marriage and Family*, (Washington, DC: Family Research Council, N.D.), 2, https://www.frc .org/brochure/the-bibles-teaching-on-marriage-and-family.

5. Gary Thomas, *Sacred Marriage: What If God Designed Marriage to Make Us Holy More than to Make Us Happy* (Grand Rapids, MI: Zondervan, 2015), 24.

6. By "occupational ministry," I mean a role, often paid and often full-time, as a leader or pastor in a church or Christian ministry.

7. NLT.

8. Protestant Episcopal Church of the U.S.A., *The Book of Common Prayer and Administration of the Sacraments and Other Rites and Ceremonies of the Church* (1789), accessed June 24, 2019, http://justus.anglican.org /resources/bcp/1789/Marriage_1789.htm.

9. Richard Fry, "New Census Data Show More Americans Are Tying the Knot, But Mostly It's the College-Educated," Pew Research Center, February 6, 2014, http://www.pewresearch.org/fact-tank/2014/02/06/new-census-data -show-more-americans-are-tying-the-knot-but-mostly-its-the-college-educated/.

10. Katelyn Beaty, *A Woman's Place: A Christian Vision for Your Calling in the Office, the Home, and the World* (New York: Howard Books, 2016), 196.

CHAPTER 5: CALLING AND SEASONS OF LIFE

1. The noted first-century Jewish historian, Josephus, has written that Samuel was around twelve years old at the time of his calling. This would also be in keeping with Jewish custom, in which a young man accompanied his parents to the Temple when he turned twelve (Luke 2:42); Josephus, *Antiquities of the Jews*, Book V, Chapter 10, Section 4, accessed July 18, 2019, www.sacred-texts.com/jud/josephus/ant-5.htm.

2. GotQuestions, "How Old Were Jesus' Disciples?,"accessed June 7, 2018, https://www.gotquestions.org/how-old-were-Jesus-disciples.html.

3. Saul McLeod, "Erik Erikson's Stages of Psychosocial Development," *Simply Psychology*, May 3, 2018, https://www.simplypsychology.org/Erik-Erikson .html.

4. Jennie Allen, *Restless: Because You Were Made for More* (Nashville: W Publishing, 2013), 64.

5. Allen, *Restless*, 65.

6. See, for example, Javier Escamilla, "The Social Security Dilemma," accessed July 26, 2019, https://web.stanford.edu/class/e297c/poverty _prejudice/soc_sec/hsocialsec.htm.

7. McLeod, "Erik Erikson's Stages of Psychosocial Development," 7.

8. Janet O. Hagberg and Robert A. Guelich, *The Critical Journey: Stages in the Life of Faith*, 2nd ed. (Salem, WI: Sheffield, 2005), 114.

9. Hagberg and Guelich, *The Critical Journey*, 119.

10. Peter Scazzero, *Emotionally Healthy Spirituality, Updated Edition* (Grand Rapids, MI: Zondervan, 2017), cover.

11. Just as we experience changes to our bodies and minds over the course of our lives, Christians also undergo changes in their spiritual lives. One of the best models to describe these stages can be found in *The Critical Journey: Stages in the Life of Faith* by Janet O. Hagberg and Robert A. Guelich.

12. Gregory Favre, "Send the Elevator Back Down," Poynter.org, November 22, 2004, https://www.poynter.org/news/send-elevator-back-down.

13. Robert Clinton, *The Making of a Leader: Recognizing the Lessons and Stages of Leadership Development*, 2nd ed. (Colorado Springs, CO: NavPress, 2015), 39.

14. Clinton, *The Making of a Leader*, 40.

15. Patricia Raybon, "Answer the Phone," in *The Wonder Years: 40 Women over 40 on Aging, Faith, Beauty, and Strength*, edited by Leslie Leyland Fields (Grand Rapids, MI: Kregel, 2018).

16. Lauren Winner, "Forty," in *The Wonder Years: 40 Women over 40 on Aging, Faith, Beauty, and Strength*.

17. Andy Stanley, "Managing Tension," *The Andy Stanley Leadership Podcast*, podcast audio, March 6, 2015, https://www.acast.com/andystanley leadershippodcast/managing-tension.

CHAPTER 6: CALLING AND MONEY

1. Mark Boyle, "How I Lived by Spending Nothing for Two Years," interview by Jessica Winch, *The Telegraph*, May 10, 2013, https://www.telegraph.co .uk/finance/personalfinance/money-saving-tips/10041544/Mark-Boyle -How-I-lived-by-spending-nothing-for-two-years.html.

2. Steve Shadrach, *The God Ask: A Fresh, Biblical Approach to Personal Support Raising* (Fayetteville, AR: CMM Press, 2013), chap. 6.

3. Other examples include Acts 4:32–5:11; 11:27-30; 1 Corinthians 16:1-2; and 2 Corinthians 8.

4. Much of the content of this section is pulled (with permission) from Angie Ward, "It's Complicated: Examining the Leader's Relationship to Money," Women Leaders, May 2, 2013, https://www.christianitytoday.com/women -leaders/2013/may/its-complicated.html.

5. Leo Sun, "A Foolish Take: Here's How Much Debt the Average U.S. Household Owes," *The Motley Fool*, November 13, 2017, https://www .fool.com/investing/2017/11/13/a-foolish-take-heres-how-much-debt-the -average-us.aspx.

6. Yonat Shimron, "More Divinity Students Leave the Master of Divinity Behind," Religion News Service, May 11, 2018, https://religionnews. com/2018/05/11/more-seminary-students-leave-the-master-of-divinity -behind/.

7. Focus on the Family, "Biblical Perspective on Debt," accessed May 28, 2018, https://www.focusonthefamily.com/family-q-and-a/life-challenges /biblical-perspective-on-debt.

8, Kenneth L. Carder, "John Wesley on Giving," *Interpreter Magazine*, July-August 2016, http://www.interpretermagazine.org/topics/john -wesley-on-giving.

9. Evelyn Clifford Urwin and Douglas Wollen, eds., *John Wesley—Christian Citizen: Selections from His Social Teaching* (London: Epworth Press, 1937), 30.

10. *Quiz Show*, directed by Robert Redford (Buena Vista, FL: Buena Vista Pictures, 1994).

11. Os Guinness, *The Call: Finding and Fulfilling God's Purpose for Your Life* (Nashville: W Publishing, 2018), 188–89.

12. Craig L. Blomberg, *Christians in an Age of Wealth: A Biblical Theology of Stewardship* (Grand Rapids, MI: Zondervan, 2013), 180.

13. Guinness, *The Call*, 271.

14. Dallas Willard, *Renovation of the Heart: Putting on the Character of Christ* (Colorado Springs: NavPress, 2012), 129.

CHAPTER 7: CALLING AND CHALLENGES

1. Douglas Stone and Sheila Heen, *Thanks for the Feedback: The Science and Art of Receiving Feedback Well* (New York: Penguin Books, 2014), 3.

2. Stone and Heen, *Thanks for the Feedback*, 16–17.

3. Os Guinness, *The Call: Finding and Fulfilling God's Purpose for Your Life* (Nashville: W Publishing, 2018), 54.

4. Beth A. Booram, *Starting Something New: Spiritual Direction for Your God-Given Dream* (Downers Grove, IL: InterVarsity Press, 2015), 33.

5. Ken Costa, *Know Your Why: Finding and Fulfilling Your Calling in Life* (Nashville: W Publishing, 2016), 73.

6. Mark Buchanan, *Spiritual Rhythm: Being with Jesus Every Season of Your Soul* (Grand Rapids, MI: Zondervan, 2010), chap. 1.

7. Buchanan, *Spiritual Rhythm*, 29.

8. Buchanan, *Spiritual Rhythm*, 40.

9. Buchanan, *Spiritual Rhythm*, 50.

10. Allen, *Restless*, 76.

11. Bill Thrall, Bruce McNichol, and Ken McElrath, *The Ascent of a Leader: How Ordinary Relationships Develop Extraordinary Character and Influence* (San Francisco: Jossey-Bass, 1999), chap. 8.

12. Mark Buchanan, *Spiritual Rhythm*, 119.

13. Gordon MacDonald, *Building Below the Waterline: Shoring Up the Foundations of Leadership* (Peabody, MA: Hendrickson, 2011), 250.

14. Costa, *Know Your Why*, 16.

15. Sharon Hodde Miller, "Why Leadership Cannot Be Your Identity," Propel Women, accessed March 20, 2018, http://www.propelwomen.org/content /why-leadership-cannot-be-your-identity/gjeb8l.

BENEDICTION

1. Richard Halvorson in Dave Henning, "Nowhere by Accident," https://www .crownofcompassion.org/2015/06/22/nowhere-by-accident/.